OTHER VOLUMES IN THIS SERIES

John Ashbery, editor, *The Best American Poetry 1988*

Donald Hall, editor, *The Best American Poetry 1989*

Jorie Graham, editor, *The Best American Poetry 1990*

Mark Strand, editor, *The Best American Poetry 1991*

Charles Simic, editor, *The Best American Poetry 1992*

Louise Glück, editor, *The Best American Poetry 1993*

A. R. Ammons, editor, *The Best American Poetry 1994*

Richard Howard, editor, *The Best American Poetry 1995*

Adrienne Rich, editor, *The Best American Poetry 1996*

James Tate, editor, *The Best American Poetry 1997*

Harold Bloom, editor, *The Best of the Best American Poetry 1988–1997*

John Hollander, editor, *The Best American Poetry 1998*

Robert Bly, editor, *The Best American Poetry 1999*

Rita Dove, editor, *The Best American Poetry 2000*

Robert Hass, editor, *The Best American Poetry 2001*

Robert Creeley, editor, *The Best American Poetry 2002*

Yusef Komunyakaa, editor, *The Best American Poetry 2003*

Lyn Hejinian, editor, *The Best American Poetry 2004*

Paul Muldoon, editor, *The Best American Poetry 2005*

Billy Collins, editor, *The Best American Poetry 2006*

Heather McHugh, editor, *The Best American Poetry 2007*

Charles Wright, editor, *The Best American Poetry 2008*

David Wagoner, editor, *The Best American Poetry 2009*

Amy Gerstler, editor, *The Best American Poetry 2010*

Kevin Young, editor, *The Best American Poetry 2011*

Mark Doty, editor, *The Best American Poetry 2012*

Robert Pinsky, editor, *The Best of the Best American Poetry: 25th Anniversary Edition*

Denise Duhamel, editor, *The Best American Poetry 2013*

THE
BEST
AMERICAN
POETRY
2014

◊　◊　◊

Terrance Hayes, Editor

David Lehman, Series Editor

SCRIBNER POETRY

NEW YORK   LONDON   TORONTO   SYDNEY   NEW DELHI

SCRIBNER POETRY
A Division of Simon & Schuster, Inc.
1230 Avenue of the Americas
New York, NY 10020

Copyright © 2014 by David Lehman
Foreword copyright © 2014 by David Lehman
Introduction copyright © 2014 by Terrance Hayes

First Scribner edition September 2014

SCRIBNER and design are registered trademarks of The Gale Group, Inc., used under license by Simon & Schuster, Inc., the publisher of this work.

For information about special discounts for bulk purchases, please contact Simon & Schuster Special Sales at 1-866-506-1949 or business@simonandschuster.com.

The Simon & Schuster Speakers Bureau can bring authors to your live event. For more information or to book an event, contact the Simon & Schuster Speakers Bureau at 1-866-248-3049 or visit our website at www.simonspeakers.com.

Jacket/cover design by Leslie Goldman
Jacket/cover art: John Sloan (American, 1871–1951), Isadora Duncan, 1911 (oil on canvas). Milwaukee Art Museum. Gift of Mr. and Mrs. Donald B. Abert. Photographed by P. Richard Eells © 2014 Delaware Art Museum / Artists Rights Society (ARS), New York.

Manufactured in the United States of America

1 3 5 7 9 10 8 6 4 2

Library of Congress Control Number: 88644281

ISBN 978-1-4767-0815-7
ISBN 978-1-4767-0817-1 (pbk)
ISBN 978-1-4767-0818-8 (ebook)

CONTENTS

Foreword by David Lehman   ix

Introduction by Terrance Hayes   xxiii

Sherman Alexie, "Sonnet, with Pride"   1

Rae Armantrout, "Control"   3

John Ashbery, "Breezeway"   5

Erin Belieu, "With Birds"   7

Linda Bierds, "On Reflection"   9

Traci Brimhall, "To Survive the Revolution"   11

Lucie Brock-Broido, "Bird, Singing"   12

Jericho Brown, "Host"   14

Kurt Brown, "Pan del Muerto"   16

CAConrad, "wondering about our demise while driving to Disneyland with abandon"   18

Anne Carson, "A Fragment of Ibykos Translated 6 Ways"   20

Joseph Ceravolo, "Hidden Bird"   25

Henri Cole, "City Horse"   26

Michael Earl Craig, "The Helmet"   27

Philip Dacey, "Juilliard Cento Sonnet"   28

Olena Kalytiak Davis, "It Is to Have or Nothing"   29

Kwame Dawes, "News from Harlem"   31

Joel Dias-Porter, "Elegy Indigo"   34

Natalie Diaz, "These Hands, if Not Gods"   36

Mark Doty, "Deep Lane"   38

Sean Thomas Dougherty, "The Blues Is a Verb"   40

Rita Dove, "The Spring Cricket Repudiates His Parable of Negritude"   42

Camille Dungy, "Conspiracy (to breathe together)"   44

Cornelius Eady, "Overturned"   46

Vievee Francis, "Fallen" 47

Ross Gay, "To the Fig Tree on 9th and Christian" 49

Eugene Gloria, "Liner Notes for Monk" 53

Ray Gonzalez, "One El Paso, Two El Paso" 55

Kathleen Graber, "The River Twice" 57

Rosemary Griggs, "SCRIPT POEM" 59

Adam Hammer, "As Like" 61

Bob Hicok, "Blue prints" 63

Le Hinton, "No Doubt About It (I Gotta Get Another Hat)" 65

Tony Hoagland, "Write Whiter" 67

Major Jackson, "OK Cupid" 69

Amaud Jamaul Johnson, "L.A. Police Chief Daryl Gates Dead at 83" 72

Douglas Kearney, "The Labor of Stagger Lee: Boar" 74

Yusef Komunyakaa, "Negritude" 75

Hailey Leithauser, "In My Last Past Life" 77

Larry Levis, "Elegy with a Darkening Trapeze inside It" 78

Gary Copeland Lilley, "Sermon of the Dreadnaught" 81

Frannie Lindsay, "Elegy for My Mother" 83

Patricia Lockwood, "Rape Joke" 85

Nathaniel Mackey, "Oldtime Ending" 90

Cate Marvin, "An Etiquette for Eyes" 96

Jamaal May, "Masticated Light" 99

Shara McCallum, "Parasol" 101

Marty McConnell, "vivisection (you're going to break my heart)" 103

Valzhyna Mort, "Sylt I" 105

Harryette Mullen, "Selection from Tanka Diary" 107

Eileen Myles, "Paint Me a Penis" 108

D. Nurkse, "Release from Stella Maris" 110

Sharon Olds, "Stanley Kunitz Ode" 111

Gregory Pardlo, "Wishing Well" 113

Kiki Petrosino, "Story Problem" 115

D. A. Powell, "See You Later." 116

Roger Reeves, "The Field Museum" 117

Donald Revell, "To Shakespeare" 118

Patrick Rosal, "You Cannot Go to the God You Love with
    Your Two Legs" 119

Mary Ruefle, "Saga" 121

Jon Sands, "Decoded" 123

Steve Scafidi, "Thank You Lord for the Dark Ablaze" 126

Frederick Seidel, "To Philip Roth, for His Eightieth" 128

Diane Seuss, "Free Beer" 130

Sandra Simonds, "I Grade Online Humanities Tests" 131

Jane Springer, "Forties War Widows, Stolen Grain" 134

Corey Van Landingham, "During the Autopsy" 135

Afaa Michael Weaver, "Passing Through Indian Territory" 137

Eleanor Wilner, "Sowing" 138

David Wojahn, "My Father's Soul Departing" 140

Greg Wrenn, "Detainment" 142

Robert Wrigley, "Blessed Are" 144

Jake Adam York, "Calendar Days" 146

Dean Young, "Emerald Spider Between Rose Thorns" 148

Rachel Zucker, "Mindful" 149

Contributors' Notes and Comments 151

Magazines Where the Poems Were First Published 195

Acknowledgments 199

David Lehman was born in New York City. Educated at Stuyvesant High School and Columbia University, he spent two years as a Kellett Fellow at Clare College, Cambridge, and worked as Lionel Trilling's research assistant upon his return from England. He is the author of nine books of poetry, including *New and Selected Poems* (2013), *Yeshiva Boys* (2009), *When a Woman Loves a Man* (2005), *The Daily Mirror* (2000), and *Valentine Place* (1996), all from Scribner. He is the editor of *The Oxford Book of American Poetry* (Oxford, 2006) and *Great American Prose Poems: From Poe to the Present* (Scribner, 2003), among other collections. *A Fine Romance: Jewish Songwriters, American Songs* (Nextbook/Schocken), the most recent of his six nonfiction books, won the Deems Taylor Award from the American Society of Composers, Authors, and Publishers (ASCAP) in 2010. Among Lehman's other books are a study in detective novels (*The Perfect Murder*), a group portrait of the New York School of poets (*The Last Avant-Garde*), and an account of the scandal sparked by the revelation that a Yale University eminence had written for a Nazi-controlled newspaper in his native Belgium (*Signs of the Times: Deconstruction and the Fall of Paul de Man*). He teaches in the graduate writing program of The New School and lives in New York City and in Ithaca, New York.

FOREWORD

by David Lehman

◊   ◊   ◊

Maybe I dreamed it. Don Draper sat sipping Canadian Club from a coffee mug on Craig Ferguson's late-night talk show. "Are you on Twitter?" the host asks. "No," Draper says. "I don't"—and here he pauses before pronouncing the distasteful verb—"tweet." Next question. "Do you read a lot of poetry?" The ad agency's creative director looks skeptical. Though the hero of *Mad Men* is seen reading Dante's *Inferno* in one season of Matthew Weiner's show and heard reciting Frank O'Hara in another, the question seems to come from left field. "Poetry isn't really celebrated any more in our culture," Don says, to which the other retorts, "It can be—if you can write in units of 140 keystrokes." Commercial break.

The laugh line reveals a shrewd insight into the subject of "poetry in the digital age," a panel-discussion perennial. The panelists agree that text messaging and Internet blogs will be seen to have exercised some sort of influence on the practice of poetry, whether on the method of composition or on the style and surface of the writing. And surely we may expect the same of a wildly popular social medium with a formal requirement as stringent as the 140-character limit. (To someone with a streak of mathematical mysticism, the relation of that number to the number of lines in a sonnet is a thing of beauty.) What Twitter offers is ultimate immediacy expressed with ultimate concision. "Whatever else Twitter is, it's a literary form," says the novelist Kathryn Schulz, who explains how easy it was for her to get addicted to "a genre in which you try to say an informative thing in an interesting way while abiding by its constraint (those famous 140 characters). For people who love that kind of challenge—and it's easy to see why writers might be overrepresented among them—Twitter has the same allure as gaming." True, the hard-to-shake habit caused its share of problems. Schulz reports a huge "distractibility increase" and other disturbing symptoms: "I have felt my *mind* get divided into tweet-size chunks." Nevertheless there is a reason that she got hooked on this "wide-ranging, intellectually stimulating, big-hearted, super fun" activity.[1] When, in an early episode of the Netflix production of *House of Cards*, one Washington journalist disparages a rival as a "Twitter twat," you know the word has arrived, and the language itself has changed to accommodate it. There are new terms ("hashtag"), acronyms ("ikr" in Detroit means "I know right?"), shorthand ("suttin" is "something" in Boston).[2] Television producers love it ("Keep those tweets coming!"). So does Wall Street: when Twitter went public in 2013, the IPO came off without a hitch, and the stock climbed with the velocity of an over-caffeinated momentum investor eager to turn a quick profit.

The desire to make a friend of the new technology is understandable, though it obliges us to overlook some major flaws: the Internet is hell on lining, spacing, italics; line breaks and indentation are often obscured in electronic transmission. The integrity of the poetic line can be a serious casualty. Still, it is fruitless to quarrel with the actuality of change, and difficult to resist it profitably—except, perhaps, in private, where we may revel in our physical books and even, if we like, write with pen or pencil on graph paper or type our thoughts with the Smith-Corona manual to which we have a sentimental attachment. One room in the fine "Drawn to Language" exhibit at the University of Southern California's Fisher Art Museum in September 2013 was devoted to Susan Silton's site-specific installation of a circle of tables on which sat ten manual typewriters of different makes, models, sizes, and decades. It was moving to behold the machines not only as objects of nostalgia in an attractive arrangement but as metonymies of the experience of writing in the twentieth century—and as invitations to sit down and hunt and peck away to your heart's content. Seeing the typewriters in that room I felt as I do when the talk touches on the acquisition of an author's papers by

1. Kathryn Schulz, "Seduced by Twitter," *The Week*, December 27, 2013, pp. 40–41.

2. Katy Steinmetz, "The Linguist's Mother Lode," *Time*, September 9, 2013, pp. 56–57. Jacob Eisenstein, a computational linguist at Georgia Tech, is quoted: "Social media has taken the informal peer-to-peer interaction that might have been almost exclusively spoken and put it in a written form. The result of that is a burst of creativity." The assumption here is that the new is necessarily "creative" in the honorific sense.

a university library. It's odd to be a member of the last generation to have "papers" in this archival and material sense. Odd for an era to slip into a museum while you watch.

You may say—I have heard the argument—that the one-minute poem is not far off. Twitter's 140-keystroke constraint—together with the value placed on being "up to speed"—brings the clock into the game. Poetry, a byte-size kind of poetry, has been, or soon will be, a benefit of attention deficit disorder. (This statement, or prediction, is not necessarily or not always made in disparagement.) Unlike the telephone, the instruments of social media rely on the written, not the spoken word, and it will be interesting to see what happens when the values of hip-hop lyricists and spoken-word poets, for whom the performative aspects of the art are paramount, tangle with the values of concision, bite, and wit consistent with the rules of the Twitter feed. On the other hand, it is conceivable that the sentence I have just composed will be, for all intents and purposes, anachronistic in a couple of years or less. Among my favorite oxymorons is "ancient computer," applied to my own desktop.[3]

★   ★   ★

In his famous and famously controversial Rede Lecture at Cambridge University in 1959, the English novelist C. P. Snow addressed the widening chasm between the two dominant strains in our culture.[4] There were the humanists on the one side. On the other were the scientists and applied scientists, the agents of technological change. And "a gulf of mutual incomprehension" separated them. Though Snow endeavored to appear evenhanded, it became apparent that he favored the sciences—he opted, in his terms, for the fact rather than the myth. The scientists "have the future in their bones"—a future that will nourish the hungry, clothe the masses, reduce the risk of infant mortality, cure ailments, and prolong life. And "the traditional culture responds by wishing the future did not exist."

3. "Even the best computer will seem positively geriatric by its fifth birthday." Geoffrey A. Fowler, "Mac Pro Is a Lamborghini, but Who Drives That Fast?" *The Wall Street Journal*, January 15, 2014, D1.

4. The 1959 Rede Lecture in four parts was published as *The Two Cultures and the Scientific Revolution*. An expanded version conjoining the lecture with Snow's subsequent reflections (*A Second Look*) appeared from Cambridge University Press in 1964.

The Rede Lecture came in the wake of the scare set off by the Soviet Union's launch of Sputnik in October 1957. There was widespread fear that we in the West, and particularly we in the United States, were in danger of falling behind the Russians in the race for space, itself a metaphor for the scientific control of the future. For this reason among others, Snow's lecture was extraordinarily successful. Introducing a phrase into common parlance, "The Two Cultures" reached great numbers of readers and helped shape a climate friendly to science at the expense of the traditional components of a liberal education. Much in that lecture infuriated the folks on the humanist side of the divide.[5] Snow wrote as though humanistic values were possible without humanistic studies. In literature he saw not a corrective or a criticism of life but a threat. He interpreted George Orwell's *1984* as "the strongest possible wish that the future should not exist" rather than as a warning against the authoritarian impulses of the modern state coupled with its sophistication of surveillance. Snow founded his argument on the unexamined assumption that scientists, in thrall to the truth, can be counted on to do the right thing—an assumption that the history of munitions would explode even if we could all agree on what "the right thing" is. For Snow, who had been knighted and would be granted a life peerage, the future was bound to be an improvement on the past, and the change would be entirely attributable to the people in the white coats in the laboratory. Generalizing from the reactionary political tendencies of certain famous modern writers, Snow floated the suggestion that they—and by implication those who read them—managed to "bring Auschwitz that much nearer." Looking back at the Rede Lecture five years later, Snow saw no reason to modify the view that intellectuals were natural Luddites, prone to "talk about a pre-Industrial Eden" that never was. They ignored the simple truth that the historian J. H. Plumb stated: "No one in his senses would choose to have been born in a previous age unless he could be certain that he would have been born into a prosperous family, that he would have enjoyed extremely good health,

5. I take the term "humanist" to cover historians and philosophers, literary and cultural critics, music and art historians, professors of English or Romance Languages or comparative literature or East Asian studies, classicists, linguists, jurists and legal scholars, public intellectuals, authors and essayists, most psychologists, and a great many other academics across the board: very nearly everyone not committed professionally to a career in one of the sciences or in technology.

and that he could have accepted stoically the death of the majority of his children." In short, according to Snow, the humanists were content to dwell in a "pretty-pretty past."

In 1962 F. R. Leavis, then perhaps the most influential literary critic at Cambridge, denounced Snow's thesis with such vitriol and contempt that he may have done the humanist side more harm than good. "Snow exposes complacently a complete ignorance," Leavis said in the Richmond Lecture, and "is as intellectually undistinguished as it is possible to be." Yet, Leavis added, Snow writes in a "tone of which one can say that, while only genius could justify it, one cannot readily think of genius adopting it."[6] Reread today, the Richmond Lecture may be a classic of invective inviting close study. As rhetoric it was devastating. But as a document in a conflict of ideas, the Richmond Lecture left much to be desired. Leavis did not adequately address the charges that Snow leveled at literature and the arts on social and moral grounds.[7] The scandal in personalities, the shrillness of tone, eclipsed the subject of the debate, which got fought out in the letters column of the literary press and was all the talk in the senior common rooms and faculty lounges of the English-speaking world.

The controversy ignited by a pair of dueling lectures at Cambridge deserves another look now not only because fifty years have passed and we can better judge what has happened in the intervening period but because more than ever the humanities today stand in need of defense. In universities and liberal arts colleges, these are hard times for the study of ideas. In 2013, front page articles in *The New York Times* and *The Wall Street Journal* screamed about the crisis in higher education especially in humanist fields: shrinking enrollments at liberal arts colleges; the shutting down of entire college departments; the elimination of courses and requirements once considered vital. The host of "worrisome long-trends" included "a national decline in the number of graduating high-school seniors, a swarm of technologies driving down costs and profit margins, rising student debt, a soft job market for college

---

6. *The Two Cultures? The Significance of C. P. Snow* by F. R Leavis.

7. For more on the affair, and an especially sensitive and sympathetic reading of Leavis's "relentlessly withering" attack on Snow, see Stefan Collini, "Leavis v. Snow: The Two-Cultures Bust-Up 50 Years On," in *The Guardian*, August 16, 2013. http://www.theguardian.com/books/2013/aug/16/leavis-snow-two-cultures-bust

graduates and stagnant household incomes."[8] Is that all? No, and it isn't everything. There has also been a spate of op-ed columns suggesting that students would be wise to save their money, study something that can lead to gainful employment, and forget about majoring in modern dance, art history, philosophy, sociology, theology, or English unless they are independently wealthy.

The cornerstones of the humanities, English and history, have taken a beating. At Yale, English was the most popular major in 1972–73. It did not make the top five in 2012–13. Twenty-one years ago, 216 Yale undergraduates majored in history; less than half that number picked the field last year.[9] Harvard—where English majors dwindled from 36 percent of the student body in 1954 to 20 percent in 2012—has issued a report on the precipitous drop. Russell A. Berman of Stanford, in a piece in *The Chronicle of Higher Education* ominously entitled "Humanist: Heal Thyself," observed that "the marginalization of the great works of the erstwhile canon has impoverished the humanities," and that the Harvard report came to this important conclusion. But he noted, too, that it stopped short of calling for a great-books list of required readings. My heart sinks when I read such a piece and arrive at a paragraph in which the topic sentence is, "Clearly majoring in the humanities has long been an anomaly for American undergraduates."[10] Or is such a sentence—constructed as if to sound value-neutral and judgment-free in the proper scientific manner—part of the problem? The ability of an educated populace to read critically, to write clearly, to think coherently, and to retain knowledge—even the ability to grasp the basic rules of grammar and diction—seems to be declining at a pace consonant with the rise of the Internet search engine and the autocorrect function in computer programs.

Not merely the cost but the value of a liberal arts education has come into doubt. The humanists find themselves in a bind. Consider the plight of the English department. "The folly of studying, say, English Lit has become something of an Internet cliché—the stuff of sneering 'Worst Majors' listicles that seem always to be sponsored by

8. Douglas Belkin, "Private Colleges Squeezed," *The Wall Street Journal*, November 10, 2013.

9. "Major Changes," *Yale Alumni Magazine*, January/February 2014, p. 20.

10. Russell A. Berman, "Humanist: Heal Thyself," *The Chronicle of Higher Education*, June 10, 2013. http://chronicle.com/blogs/conversation/2013/06/10/humanist-heal-thyself/

personal-finance websites," Thomas Frank writes in *Harper's*.[11] There is a new philistinism afoot, and the daunting price tag of college or graduate education adds an extra wrinkle to an argument of ferocious intensity. "The study of literature has traditionally been felt to have a unique effectiveness in opening the mind and illuminating it, in purging the mind of prejudices and received ideas, in making the mind free and active," Lionel Trilling wrote at the time of the Leavis–Snow controversy. "The classic defense of literary study holds that, from the effect which the study of literature has upon the private sentiments of a student, there results, or can be made to result, an improvement in the intelligence, and especially the intelligence as it touches the moral life."[12] It is vastly more difficult today to mount such a defense after three or more decades of sustained assault on canons of judgment, the idea of greatness, the related idea of genius, and the whole vast cavalcade of Western civilization.[13] Heather Mac Donald writes more in sorrow than in anger that the once-proud English department at UCLA— which even lately could boast of being home to more undergraduate majors than any other department in the nation—has dismantled its core, doing away with the formerly obligatory four courses in Chaucer, Shakespeare, and Milton. You can now satisfy the requirements of an English major with "alternative rubrics of gender, sexuality, race, and class." The coup, as Mac Donald terms it, took place in 2011 and is but

11. Thomas Frank, "Course Corrections," *Harper's Magazine*, October 2013, p. 10. The editorial writers of the *New York Post* begin a *defense* of the liberal arts with "the nightmare scenario for many parents of college students. Suzie comes home from her $50,000-a-year university to tell you this: 'Mom and Dad, I've decided I want to major in early Renaissance poetry.' " *New York Post*, February 22, 2014.

12. Lionel Trilling, "The Two Environments: Reflections on the Study of English," in *Beyond Culture* (1965; rpt. New York: Harcourt Brace Jovanovich, 1978), p. 184. See also Trilling's lucid account of the Leavis–Snow controversy in the same volume, pp. 126–54.

13. "In according the least legitimacy to the word 'genius,' one is considered to sign one's resignation from all fields of knowledge," Jacques Derrida said in 2003. The very noun, he said, "makes us squirm." At the same time that academics banished the word, magazines such as *Time* and *Esquire* began to dumb it down, applying "genius" to all manner of folk, including fashion designers, corporate executives, performers, comedians, talk-show hosts, and even point guards who shoot too much (Allen Iverson, circa 2000). See Darrin M. McMahon, "Where Have All the Geniuses Gone?" in *The Chronicle Review*, October 21, 2013. http://chronicle.com/article/Where-Have-All-the-Geniuses/142353/

one event in a pattern of academic changes that would replace a theory of education based on a "constant, sophisticated dialogue between past and present" with a consumer mind-set based on "narcissism, an obsession with victimhood, and a relentless determination to reduce the stunning complexity of the past to the shallow categories of identity and class politics. Sitting atop an entire civilization of aesthetic wonders, the contemporary academic wants only to study oppression, preferably his or her own, defined reductively according to gonads and melanin."[14]

In the antagonism between science and the humanities, it may now be said that C. P. Snow in "The Two Cultures" was certainly right in one particular. Technology in our culture has routed the humanities. Everyone wants the latest app, the best device, the slickest new gadget. Put on the defensive, spokespersons for the humanities have failed to make an effective case for their fields of study. There have been efforts to promote the digital humanities, it being understood that the adjective "digital" is what rescues "humanities" in the phrase. Has the faculty thrown in the towel too soon? Have literature departments and libraries welcomed the end of the book with unseemly haste? Have the conservators of culture embraced the acceleration of change that may endanger the study of the literary humanities as if—like the clock face, cursive script, and the rotary phone—it, too, can be effectively consigned to the ash heap of the analog era?

There is some resistance to the tyranny of technology, the ruthlessness of the new digital media. And in the incipient resistance, there is the resort to culture as we traditionally knew it—the poem on the printed page, the picture in the gallery, the concerto in the symphony hall. "There is no greater bulwark against the twittering acceleration of American consciousness than the encounter with a work of art, and the experience of a text or an image," Leon Wieseltier told the graduating class at Brandeis University in May 2013. Wieseltier, the longtime literary editor of *The New Republic*, feels the situation is dire. "In the digital universe, knowledge is reduced to the status of information." In truth, however, "knowledge can be acquired only over time and only by method. And the devices that we carry like addicts in our hands are disfiguring our mental lives." Let us not be so quick to jettison the monuments of unaging intellect. "There is no task more urgent in

14. Heather Mac Donald, "The Humanities Have Forgotten Their Humanity," *The Wall Street Journal*, January 3, 2014. http://online.wsj.com/news/articles/SB10001424052702304858104579264321265378790

American intellectual life at this hour than to offer some resistance to the twin imperialisms of science and technology."[15]

★ ★ ★

One thing you can count on is that people will keep writing as they adjust from one medium to another, analog to digital, paper to computer monitor. Upon the appearance of the 2004 edition of *The Best American Poetry* (ed. Lyn Hejinian), David Orr wrote that the series stands for "the idea of poetry as a community activity. 'People are writing poems!' each volume cries. 'You, too, could write a poem!' It's an appealingly democratic pose, and it has always been the genuinely 'best' thing about the Best American series."[16] Is everyone a poet?[17] It was Freud who laid the intellectual foundations for the idea. He argued that each of us is a poet when dreaming or making wisecracks or even when making slips of the tongue or pen. If daydreaming is a passive form of creative writing, it follows that the unconscious to which we all have access is the content provider, and what is left to learn is technique. It took the advent of creative writing as an academic field to institutionalize what might be a natural tendency in American democracy. In the proliferation of competent poems, poems that meet a certain standard of artistic finish but may lack staying power, I cannot see much harm except to note one inevitable consequence, which is that of inflation. In economics, inflation takes the form of a devaluation of currency. In poetry, inflation lessens the value that the culture attaches to any individual poem. But this is far from a new development. Byron in a journal entry in 1821 or 1822 captured the economic model with his customary brio: "there are *more* poets (soi-disant) than ever there were, and proportionally *less* poetry."[18]

15. Leon Wieseltier, "Perhaps Culture Is Now the Counterculture," *The New Republic*, May 28, 2013. http://www.newrepublic.com/article/113299/leon-wieseltier-commencement-speech-brandeis-university-2013

16. David Orr, "The Best American Poetry 2004: You, Too, Could Write a Poem." *The New York Times Book Review*, November 21, 2004.

17. Madeline Schwartzman, an adjunct professor of architecture at Barnard College, is stopping someone on the subway every day and asking the person to write a poem on the spot for "365 Day Subway: Poems by New Yorkers." Heidi Mitchell, "Artist Solicits Poetry from Other Subterraneans," *The Wall Street Journal*, February 1–2, 2014, A15.

18. Byron, "Detached Thoughts" (October 1821 to May 1822), in *Byron's Poetry*, ed. Frank D. McConnell (W. W. Norton, 1978), p. 335.

Another thing you can count on: at seemingly regular intervals an article will appear in a wide-circulation periodical declaring—as if it hasn't been said often before—that poetry is finished, kaput, dead, and what are they doing with the corpse? Back in 1888, Walt Whitman read an article forecasting the demise of poetry in fifty years "owing to the special tendency to science and to its all-devouring force." (Whitman's comment: "I anticipate the very contrary. Only a firmer, vastly broader, new area begins to exist—nay, is already formed—to which the poetic genius must emigrate.")[19] In his introduction to *The Sacred Wood* (1920), T. S. Eliot ridiculed the kind of argument encountered in fashionable London circles of the day. Edmund Gosse had written in the *Sunday Times*: "Poetry is not a formula which a thousand flappers and hobble-dehoys ought to be able to master in a week without any training, and the mere fact that it seems to be now practiced with such universal ease is enough to prove that something has gone amiss with our standards." Here is Eliot's paraphrase of the Gosse argument: "If too much bad verse is published in London, it does not occur to us to raise our standards, to do anything to educate the poetasters; the remedy is, Kill them off." (Eliot also asks: "is it wholly the fault of the younger generation that it is aware of no authority that it must respect?")[20] On occasion the death-of-poetry genre can produce something useful; Edmund Wilson's essay "Is Verse a Dying Technique?" comes to mind. But today you are more likely to find "Poetry and Me: An Elegy."

In its July 2013 issue, *Harper's* published a typical example of the genre, Mark Edmundson's "Poetry Slam: Or, The Decline of American Verse."[21] The piece by an older academic bewailing the state of something he calls "mainstream American poetry" and praising the poetry he loved as a youth is embarrassing for what it reveals about the author, who is out of touch with the poetry in circulation. And then "mainstream American poetry" is poor turf to stand on: Would you offer a course with that label? Would anyone want to fit into such a category? The professor's chief complaint appears to be that "there's no end of poetry being written and published out there," and though he knows he shouldn't generalize, he will do just that and say that today's

19. Whitman in "A Backward Glance O'er Travel'd Roads" (1888), in *Walt Whitman: A Critical Anthology*, ed. Francis Murphy (Penguin, 1969), pp. 110–11.
20. Eliot, *The Sacred Wood* (1920; rpt. Methuen, 1960), p. xv.
21. *Harper's Magazine*, July 2013, pp. 61–68.

poets lack ambition—"the poets who now get the balance of public attention and esteem are casting unambitious spells," which is at least a grudging acknowledgment, if only by virtue of the metaphor, that our poets remain magicians.

When such a piece runs, the magazine subsequently prints a handful of the letters the offending article has provoked. Of the three letters that *Harper's* saw fit to print in its September 2013 issue, one writer was vexed that Edmundson had focused "almost exclusively" on white males. A second thought it a shame that the author had overlooked the work of hip-hop lyricists (such as Kendrick Lamar and Nas). The third letter was written by Harvard Professor Stephen Burt, an assiduous critic and reader. He pointed out that there is "something bullying" in the call for "public" poetry. Whose public, he asked: "A public poem, in Edmundson's view, might be an interest-group poem whose collective has a flag." Attacks on contemporary American poetry such as Edmundson's "have been made for centuries" and are best seen as "screeds [that] create an opportunity for those of us who read a lot of poetry to recommend individual poets as we come to poetry-in-general's defense."[22]

Each year in *The Best American Poetry* we seize that opportunity and ask a distinguished poet to glean the harvest of poems and identify the ones he or she thinks best. Terrance Hayes has undertaken the task with vigor and inventiveness. A native of South Carolina, Hayes went to Coker College on a basketball scholarship, studied the visual arts, and wrote poetry on the side. An instructor directed him to the MFA poetry program at the University of Pittsburgh, where he studied with Toi Derricotte and joined Cave Canem, the organization that has done so much to nourish the remarkable generation of African American poets on the scene today. Terrance won the 2010 National Book Award for his book *Lighthead* (Penguin). His poems—which have appeared seven times in *The Best American Poetry*—reflect a deep interest in matters of masculinity, sexuality, and race; a flair for narrative; and a love of verbal games as the key to ad hoc forms and procedures. I was thrilled when Hayes told me that the first book of poems he ever acquired was the 1990 edition of *The Best American Poetry*, Jorie Graham's volume, and that he owns all the books in the series. When I asked him to read for the 2014 book, I had in front of me the winter 2010–11 issue of

22. *Harper's Magazine*, September 2013, pp. 2–3.

Ploughshares, which Hayes edited. In his introduction, he wrote about a notional three-story museum, the "Sentenced Museum," which resembles an inverted pyramid with the literature of self-reflection on the ground floor, the language of witness one flight up, and a host of "tangential parlors, wings and galleries" on the third and largest floor. I remember reading the issue and thinking, "as an editor, he's a natural."

As ever, this year's volume includes our elaborate back-of-the-book apparatus. To the value of the comments the poets make on the work chosen for this book, the poets themselves attest. In the 2013 edition, Dorianne Laux comments on her "Song," "Death permeates the poem, which wasn't apparent to me until I was asked to write this paragraph."

★　★　★

It used to be the death of God that got all the attention—God whose decomposing corpse made the big stink. Was it, in the end, Nietzsche, Freud, *Time* magazine, or the masses (who preferred, in the end, other opiates) that did Him in? I can't say, but I take solace in knowing that there are, besides myself, other holdouts refusing to suspend their belief. Meanwhile, the subject has receded to the terrorism and fundamentalism pages of your newspaper, and the focus has long since shifted to literature. The death of the novel worried all-star committees for years. There was a split decision that satisfied no one, and now, with Updike dead and Roth retired, a new consensus is starting to form around the notion that the TV serial as exemplified by *The Sopranos*, *Mad Men*, *Breaking Bad*, *House of Cards*, and *Homeland* has supplanted not only the novel but the movie as a mass entertainment form—one that can aspire to be both wildly popular and notably artistic, as the novel was at its best. The past tense in that last clause makes me sad, though I have seen the future and it is even more enthralling than Galsworthy's *Forsyte Saga* given the *Masterpiece Theatre* treatment with Damian Lewis as Soames.

As to poetry, is it dead, does it matter, is there too much of it, does anyone anywhere buy books of poetry? The discussion is fraught with anxiety and perhaps that implies a love of poetry, and a longing for it, and a fear that we may be in danger of losing it if we do not take care to promote it, teach it well, and help it reach the reader whose life depends on it. Will magazine editors continue to fall for a pitch lamenting that poetry has become a "small-time game," that it is "too hermetic," or "programmatically obscure," lacking ambition and public spiritedness? The lack of originality is no bar. Think of how many issues of finance magazines are identical in their contents year after year. Retire at sixty-five. Insider tips from the pros. What to do about bonds in 2014 "and beyond." Why it makes dollars and sense to "ditch cable." Or consider the general audience magazine, editors of which will not soon tire of running articles that contend that a woman today either can or cannot "have it all." I am so sure that death-of-poetry pronouncements will continue to be made that I am tempted to assign the task as a writing exercise. It's an evergreen.

Terrance Hayes was born in Columbia, South Carolina, in 1971. He was educated at Coker College, where he studied painting and English and was an Academic All-American on the men's basketball team. After receiving his MFA in poetry from the University of Pittsburgh in 1997, he taught in southern Japan; Columbus, Ohio; and New Orleans, Louisiana. Hayes returned to Pittsburgh in 2001 and taught for twelve years at Carnegie Mellon University before joining the faculty of the University of Pittsburgh in the fall of 2013. He is the author of *Lighthead* (Penguin Books, 2010), winner of the 2010 National Book Award and finalist for the National Book Critics Circle Award. His first book, *Muscular Music* (Tia Chucha Press, 1999), won both a Whiting Writers' Award and the Kate Tufts Discovery Award. His second book, *Hip Logic* (Penguin, 2002), was a National Poetry Series selection and a finalist for both the *Los Angeles Times* Book Prize and the James Laughlin Award from the Academy of American Poets. *Wind in a Box* (Penguin, 2006), a Hurston-Wright Legacy Award finalist, was named one of the best books of 2006 by *Publishers Weekly*, whose reviewer wrote: "In his hip, funny, yet no less high-stakes third collection, Hayes solidifies his reputation as one of the best poets—African American or otherwise—now writing." He has also received a National Endowment for the Arts Fellowship, a United States Artists Zell Fellowship, and a Guggenheim Fellowship. *How to Be Drawn*, Hayes's new collection of poems, is forthcoming from Penguin in 2015.

INTRODUCTION

by Terrance Hayes

◊　◊　◊

"What we end up making, whether it's something we do by
ourselves or with others, is always a form of conversation."
—Eugene Gloria

Terrance Hayes begins his introduction to the 2014 edition of *The
Best American Poetry* with a recollection of the first poetry book he ever
purchased. Some manner of luck, he tells us, led him to the sole shelf
of poetry in the sole bookstore of his very small college in a very small
town in rural South Carolina. The book, Jorie Graham's 1990 edi-
tion of *The Best American Poetry*, became his first contemporary poetry
teacher. "I am a proud mutt of poetic influences, having been reared
by seventy-five parents," Hayes begins in a passage that goes on to
elaborate (for six pages) the ways those poets and indeed the poets of
every edition of *The Best American Poetry* anthology (Hayes owns them
all) represent a "unity of contradictions," a gathering of styles proving,
one after the other, year after year, just how resistant a contemporary
American poem and contemporary American poet can be to any homo-
geneous notion of American poetry.

Let me pause here to comment on Hayes's massive introduction.
Having read the *Best American Poetry* series so closely—having depended
on it so deeply for literally all of his life as a poet—he naturally had
much to say. In the end he sent the gargantuan text to me (I am a prac-
ticed poetry scholar and literary advisor) for feedback. So unwieldy
was his 182-page introduction that it promptly "unwielded" my com-
mentary! (I returned it to Hayes with thirty pages of suggestions.)
What follows in lieu of the introduction is my interview with Hayes
about poetry, poetry introductions, introductions to poetry, and art in
general.

—Dr. Charles Kinbote

Dr. Kinbote: It is a graupelous December evening and I am with Terrance Hayes in the wine and coffee shop of a quaint American neighborhood. Before we go too far, what explanation or polite excuse can you offer regarding this unconventional "interview as introduction"?

Terrance Hayes: David Foster Wallace argues in his intro to the 2007 *Best American Essays* that since the guest editor's introduction is rarely of interest to a reader, the editor has some freedom to do and play as he pleases. I thought I'd test that theory. I thought inviting your scholarly assistance could spice things up. Thanks for agreeing to help me with this.

CK: No one ever accused scholars of being less wordy than artists, of course! But I am glad this format will allow a more succinct conversation.

TH: Initially, I thought editing this collection would be similar to guest editing a poetry journal, but it was at least three or four times more challenging. I found myself obsessing over the concept of "best." I wanted to include the best poems by established as well as emerging poets. I wanted to include the best poems from various regions of the country, the best poem in print, the best online poem, the best formal poem, the best experimental poem—I was on an overwhelming hunt for the best "knowns" and "unknowns." I wanted to base my choices on something other than taste, but I don't know if I found one. . . .

CK: Your introduction goes to *great* lengths about such things. Perhaps it is a kind of Don't-Blame-Me-If-You-Don't-Like-These-Poems flag of surrender?

TH: No, no exactly. There are all kinds of bests, I realized, just as virtually every *Best American Poetry* guest editor before me has acknowledged.

CK: To whom, then, should the task of naming *the best* fall? Critics, publishers, poetry teachers? Students of poetry teachers? NPR listeners, magazine subscribers? Other poets and poetic coteries? Is a poet better equipped than a nonpoet to appreciate poetry? Many seem to believe so.

TH: Nonpoets—not just readers who aren't poets, but even other writers and writing teachers—assume near total ignorance when it comes to contemporary poetry. But I believe a reader knows good poetry when she encounters it. You know when a poem moves you just as you know when good music moves you, regardless of its genre or style. The problems arise when we are asked to explain *why we like what we like*. It's a problem for everyone, save a few deluded scholars, I guess.

CK: Ha! Let us toast the grand delusion of expertise!

TH: Sure thing. I can't say I "literally" understand Rae Armantrout's poem "Control" or Kiki Petrosino's "Story Problem," but I love the "hunch" those poems spark. I love the moment of "not knowing" more than the moment of "knowing" in a poem.

CK: That sounds a bit like Keats's Negative Capability. And, of course, one example of Negative Capability is accepting that one cannot define Negative Capability. Tell me: how do you *judge* something you do not understand? How does anyone value something he does not understand?

TH: That could describe Man's relationship to God: the process of engaging a force you can never understand. Mystery is good enough for religion, why can't it be good enough for poetry? And who says poetry is about *understanding*, anyway? Flannery O'Connor says it is the business of literature to embody mystery.

CK: She says that of "fiction," not poetry. She is referencing a Henry James comment—

TH: Right. She says the mystery of our lives on earth is the work of—let's just say *Art*. I have the quote here on my smartphone: "manners are those conventions which, in the hands of the artist, reveal that central mystery."

CK: Ah, but don't unhip words like "manners" and "conventions" make you bristle?

TH: I take them to be synonyms for "craft." Language is figurative when it has *shape*. Language casts a shadow when it has shape. You can't give it shape without setting it in some manner of *craft*.

CK: Are you thinking of Martin Heidegger in *Poetry, Language, Thought* here? You must be!

TH [A sort of diagonal "yes" nod and "no" shake issues]: Heidegger?

CK: His theory of throwness (*geworfenheit*) and projection (*entwurf*) in Art? "Art then is the becoming and the happening of truth," Heidegger says. Which I take to mean that Art evidences our material *thatness*, on the one hand, and the possibility of our immaterial *thereness* on the other. Is this what you are suggesting?

TH: That sounds interesting. What did you say was the name of the book?

CK: I will write it down for you. I am asking if you believe that poetry,

TH: the poetry of our contemporary moment, apropos of this anthology, has any relationship to philosophy, to Truth with a capital T?

TH: Wow, hard question.

CK: My sense of contemporary poetry is generally one in which the poet is diligently hacking a path through a thicket of tangled language—I only ask that he look over his shoulder occasionally to assure us readers he knows we're behind him. It is essentially the glance Orpheus flashed Eurydice that a reader requires.

TH: Well, we know how that turned out for Eurydice—but certainly I agree: a writer hopes his readers are following.

CK: And what is it that you think readers want from poetry, from literature, from Art?

TH: Every reader comes with a different desire, I guess. Every poem offers a different gift. An interested reader need only come armed with curiosity and generosity. Openness. I wouldn't even require "patience." If the poem can't keep you in your seat, get up. Maybe come back later.

CK: I disagree. Poetry being *poetry* does indeed demand patience. The task of critics like myself is to show readers the value of remaining in their seats. We are not unlike clergymen in this way. We are not always loyal to the text, but we are always faithful to it. Apologies, apologies: I'm preaching. I digress as I said I would not. Would you like another glass of wine?

TH: OK.

CK: Your introduction also talks extensively about themes in contemporary poetry.

TH: Yes, I inevitably gave up trying to explain the significance of certain recurring themes in the collection, and instead made centos reflecting the themes. Each cento consists of lines culled exclusively from poems in this book. There are three in the introduction: "The Sex Cento," "The Political Cento," and "The Death Cento."

CK: "Cento" from the Greek, *kentron*: patchwork? A poem built from the writings of other authors, yes? A humorless quodlibet, the form seems to me. Shall we hear the sex cento?

TH: All right, but don't ask me to explain it:

SEX CENTO

I, too, love the devil. | It is hard to have faith in this. | I am not smart about love, is what I'm saying | I pray without speech. |

that's the price the wind pays. | Even if you don't know how it feels to fall, you can get my drift | the sweet, sweet air as it makes its way around the curve | If the best thing the world discovered today is that at the inside of the universe is a cat | The water is flat like fur licked down by a clean animal | Yes, I am anthropomorphizing goddammit | I'm a hog for you baby | what we end up making, whether it's something we do by ourselves or with others, is always a form of conversation. | I will never contain the whole of it.

CK: "I, too, love the devil," from the opening of Traci Brimhall's quite memorable poem—I heard that in there. From what poem is "If the best thing the world discovered today is that at the inside of the universe is a cat" excerpted?

TH: That's from Eileen Myles's poem, "Paint Me a Penis."

CK: Clever, yes, but I am still on the fence about these little postmodern desipiences.

TH: What does "desipience" mean?

CK: As Horace says in "Ode 12" of Book IV of *The Odes*: "Dulce est desipere in loco." It is pleasant to be frivolous on occasion.

TH: I wasn't trying to be frivolous. I have an actual theory—well, I'm working on a theory about *heat* in a poem, the charge of its language. In my classes I ask students to name a poem's hot spots. The idea is that in any poem there is a line or two that heats the rest of the poem. A kind of focal point that both anchors and charges it. The centos are compiled of hot spots in the poems collected here.

CK: I see. There is a similar "linguistic fleetness" in many poems. In Steve Scafidi's "Thank You Lord for the Dark Ablaze," Sandra Simonds's "I Grade Online Humanities Tests," and Rachel Zucker's "Mindful"—where we actually see "GO GO GO GO"—there is a similarly animated, scantily punctuated syntax. Was one such poem not enough? I think these poems reveal your biases, Mr. Hayes, your limited tastes.

TH: These poems are very different, Doctor, although I do find "linguistic fleetness" appealing in general . . . "Velocity" is a good word. Velocity of mind and tongue and feeling. Maybe I'm limited by my penchant for what Frank O'Hara called *Personism*. I don't mind a poem of more meditative intensity, though. The David Wojahn poem, "My Father's Soul Departing," comes to mind.

CK: I should not be drinking both red wine and espresso at this hour.

TH: Often I can look a poem in its mouth and find its sounds are beautiful, but the question is inevitably, "Am I always drawn to the same music?" As I selected poems, I often asked myself whether others would hear the music I heard. Ultimately, I can't be sure readers will agree with what's superlative here. I can only let the poems speak for themselves.

CK: James Dickey, on the first day of his classes, I was once told, often climbed onto what was surely a very strong table, oak most likely, and into what was surely a very strong chair, and declared to his pupils: "Now ask me any question about life and I will answer it using this book!" He usually held a book of Shakespeare, the sonnets, the plays—I am told it worked every time. Could you perform such a feat with *this* book?

TH [frowning and fidgeting for a spell]: Yes.

CK: Perhaps later, then, we shall try it out. Your introduction includes a few pages discussing poems left on the cutting-room floor. Is there one in particular that you wish you had included?

TH: A poem by the late Alan Dugan. It came late in the year from *Ploughshares*. I'm cheating a little to include it outside the table of contents:

PRIAPUS

I am the only man in the world
because I have no tits. I have
a permanent hard-on as long
as I am tall and it
outweighs me.
                    They say that I
have horns, hooves, and a tail, but this
is a myth or a lie: my forehead
is knobbed, my coccyx is protuberant,
and my toes are flanged.
                              Most
people run away when I walk down the street,
but some of the women tear off their clothes
fall down on their backs and open their legs
as far as they can and scream "Fuck me,"
and some of the little boys drop their pants,
bend over and spread their cheeks

and yell "Do me! Mister, do me!"

They say

that I have wings to fly me away from all

this obscenity, and that

they are either on my organ or on my back,

but this is a myth or not,

so come to the towns of northern Greece

or bloody Macedonia on your vacation,

and find out.

CK: The little boys yell, "Do me, Mister"?

TH: It's a ballsy poem, right? You know who Priapus was? He was the minor god with the big—

CK: Yes, yes, I know who Priapus was! Let us change the subject. There are a few diagrams and illustrations in your introduction. The poem by Michael Earl Craig, for example, is accompanied by what looks like an ornate map of roads around a hat-shaped city. Take a look at this diagram by Jacques Maritain from his chapter, "The Internalization of Music" in *Creative Intuition in Art and Poetry*:

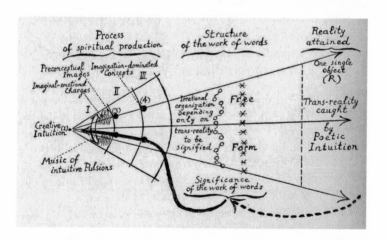

Maritain describes this as an illustration of creative intuition in search of expression in modern poetry. Can you offer some thoughts regarding your own diagrams?

TH: I hope my drawings aren't quite that complicated. I admire Maritain's effort to demystify poetry. Words fail, so he resorts to diagrams. Ironically, things remain bewildering even drawn out. What does he mean by "process of spiritual production" and the "structure of the work of words," for example?

CK: "The creative process is free to start developing in the nest of dynamic unity of image and thought where the music of intuitive pulsions takes place, and where emotion and nascent images are pregnant with virtual intelligibility," Maritain says. The diagram makes this quite clear.

TH: The diagrams in my introduction are sort of tongue-in-cheek. When I realized I couldn't explain what makes a poem great, I thought I'd try illustrating it. "Show don't tell." Something like that.

CK: You have picked several poems written in ad hoc forms. I am thinking of Rosemary Griggs's "SCRIPT POEM," Anne Carson's "A Fragment of Ibykos Translated 6 Ways," and Sherman Alexie's subversive "Sonnet, with Pride." But there are poems in "pre-established forms" as well. Linda Bierds's "On Reflection" is a pantoum, Hailey Leithauser's "In My Last Past Life" is a villanelle. Philip Dacey's "Juilliard Cento Sonnet" is both cento and sonnet. If I ask you to explain this, I am sure you will say, "A good poem is a good poem," or some such platitude.

TH: A good poem *is* a good poem.

CK: Instead I would like you to address the diversity that seems more than anything to have guided your decisions. A formal poem here, an experimental poem there, a poem by a "person of color" here, a poem by an old white guy there—how is anyone to really understand the essence of "American Poetry" if it amounts to a *gumbo* and *get-along* of choices?

TH: Some might say memory is the soul of imagination; that we seldom can imagine something before we have remembered an experience of it, a sense of it.

CK: Who says that?

TH [ignoring the question]: But let's consider diversity as possibly the soul of imagination. I'm not ashamed to say I wanted a diverse mix. In my introduction I describe my poetic tastes as something like a yard with a fence I cannot see. If I leave my porch and walk over a few hills, cross a few rivers, I suspect I will find my border: the place where I say *this is a poem, this is not.* But ultimately, I want my yard to be bigger not smaller, and this editing process made that possible. Still, I'm sure you can find styles or schools I left out.

CK: Some of your choices could be construed as political. I am reminded of Harold Bloom's pugnacious introduction to *The Best of the Best American Poetry 1988–1997* wherein—

TH: Where while decrying political poetry, Bloom writes one of the most political introductions in the series—

CK: Is that how you read his introduction?

TH: I'll stick with my fenced yard analogy. Bloom's fence comes right up to his door. Which would be fine if he wasn't such an anxious neighbor—the sort who not only confiscates the balls inadvertently tossed inside his fence, but also means to outlaw any ball games he doesn't recognize.

CK: Bloom's fervor is admirable. Like me, he is one of the few scholars paying attention to contemporary poetry. What, it must be asked, do you think is the function of the critic in an ever-uncritical culture?

TH: I don't mind critics. That's why you're here in advance of the critics and reviewers at the door. But do we really need someone to police the boundaries of poetry? I'm not saying that Adrienne Rich's 1996 volume was, like, the best of the best, but Bloom became narrow and polemical as he accused Rich of being narrow and polemical. It just wasn't a very generous introduction. If there is no generosity toward the arts, there is no Art.

CK: Fine. I happen to think Bloom is invaluable to poets. But enough of that. You have a political cento in your introduction. Let's hear that one before I order another bottle of wine. The Argentinian Malbec?

TH:

POLITICAL CENTO

It takes an American to do really big things. | For just a moment, imagine yourself as an Iraqi living in Baghdad. | dance backward toward town, down the long dirt road | Attack, back off, and then | GO GO GO GO | I believe in life as sure as I believe in death | I know why he is in ache. | How can a piece of knowledge be stupid | It's all Romeo and Juliet—hate crimes, booty calls, political assassinations. | All thumbs. All bicoastal and discreet and masculine and muscular. | so much to be learned and even more to be researched. | I know some readers need to see their lives reflected on the page | I'll spend the rest of the week closing an eye to the world | Let that be true.

CK: Well. I don't know how "political" that is. But you also selected a poem inspired by the Trayvon Martin story: Jon Sands's "Decoded."

TH: Yes, that's a terrific poem.

CK: Is it not too topical?

TH: It's ingeniously structured. It shows us just how complicated a political poem—I don't think I trust that descriptor—can be. Actually, I think Patricia Lockwood's "Rape Joke" is more controversial.

CK: We should talk about that one.

TH: I'm not sure what to say about it. There's so much to say about it. Which is why it's here speaking for itself.

CK: So we're not going to talk about it?

TH: Listen, a dude can't really cheer for a poem called "Rape Joke." But what I felt reading it is akin to what I feel reading poems white people sometimes write about race. I'm thinking especially of Eleanor Wilner's "Sowing," or Tony Hoagland's poem, "Write Whiter." A reader can call for silence when a poem engages taboo subjects, or a reader can call for conversation. "Rape Joke" calls for conversation.

CK: Soon our opinions will realign, Terrance. I have faith.

TH: It's OK with me if they don't.

CK: Here is the opening sentence of Italo Calvino's essay, "Definitions of Territories: Eroticism": "Sexuality in literature is a language in which what is not said is more important than what is." Does this hold true for poetry as well?

TH: Gerhard Richter says something similar: that painting shows what isn't there. So maybe it's a better general statement about the effort of Art to make the immaterial material? Lockwood's poem does that. As does Joseph Ceravolo's "Hidden Bird." But such big declarations about Art, even when it's Richter or Calvino positing them, are always slippery. Rothko was making fun of rules even as he offered a fairly palatable recipe for Art in his 1958 lecture at the Pratt Institute:

1. There must be a clear preoccupation with death—intimations of mortality. . . . Tragic art, romantic art, etc., deals with the knowledge of death.
2. Sensuality. Our basis of being concrete about the world. It is a lustful relationship to things that exist.

3. Tension. Either conflict or curbed desire.
4. Irony. This is a modern ingredient—the self-effacement and examination by which a man for an instant can go on to something else.
5. Wit and Play . . . for the human element.
6. The ephemeral and chance . . . for the human element.
7. Hope. 10% to make the tragic concept more endurable.

It's a pretty good recipe for poetry.

CK: Certainly there are poems preoccupied with death. Mark Doty in "Deep Lane," Sharon Olds's elegiac "Stanley Kunitz Ode," Corey Van Landingham's "During the Autopsy." You have more poems by dead poets than most of the anthologies in this series: Kurt Brown, Joseph Ceravolo, Adam Hammer, Larry Levis, Jake Adam York. Interestingly, all of them are deceased *white male poets*. Is this to suggest the white male poet is a dying breed?

TH [laughing]: Of course not! You really shouldn't be drinking red wine and espresso.

CK: What are we to make of the specter of death in poetry? Seems the hour is always elegiac, the heart cries out.

TH: I remember something the poet John Shade said once. I'm sure you remember because he said it to you: "Life is a great surprise. I do not see why death should not be an even greater one."

CK: You, Mr. Hayes, are no John Shade. I pray you do not find this fact offensive.

TH: That's cool. Sorry I brought him up. Seems like a good time to read the "Death Cento":

DEATH CENTO

There is a double heart behind the breast bone. | In particular, there is a rift through everything | You/I take/nurture my/your | I live alone with my life | I have come to believe in loss as a way of knowing | for dying is a song the body is learning | the choir shouts Praise! Stand up and be forgiven | It is customary to hold the dead in your mouth | One must at times learn to ignore the body | I mean, what good are words | they strapped me to a steel table and told me to recite the poem that would save the world | I tell them to imagine me on horseback | It takes a while to sort it out | it kisses me goodbye. I'm dead. (Pause). | How absurd to still have a body

CK: Shall we end there? With death? It is a tad depressing, I think.

TH: We can end with the opposite of death. Something you said once: "I shall continue to exist. I may assume other disguises, other forms, but I shall try to exist." It's akin to the act and ambition of making poems—all Art-making. The desire to change as well as endure.

CK: I am flattered. Let us end, then, with what this interview is not. What this is not, you realize, is your 182-page introduction decorated in graphs, poetic astrologies, recipes, explications, photos, theories on Art and Poetry and America. . . . You implied at the outset that introductions matter little. Doesn't a bit of judgment improve, and if we are lucky, refine the mind? You might be cutting corners, Sir. Poetry like all Art demands a bit of selectivity.

TH: I think I've been selective, Dr. Kinbote. The poems are here as proof. They are a gift to you whom I was thinking of all along the way. How you might, on an overcast day, criticize my choices. How you might, on a well-lit day, salute what I salute, and be transformed as I have been transformed.

THE
BEST
AMERICAN
POETRY
2014

SHERMAN ALEXIE

Sonnet, with Pride

◇ ◇ ◇

Inspired by *Pride of Baghdad*
by Brian K. Vaughan & Niko Henrichon

1. In 2003, during the Iraq War, a pride of lions escaped from the
Baghdad Zoo during an American bombing raid. 2. Confused, injured,
unexpectedly free, the lions roamed the streets searching for food and
safety. 3. For just a moment, imagine yourself as an Iraqi living in
Baghdad. You are running for cover as the U.S. bombers, like metal
pterodactyls, roar overhead. You are running for cover as some of
your fellow citizens, armed and angry, fire rifles, rocket launchers, and
mortars into the sky. You are running for cover as people are dying all
around you. It's war, war, war. And then you turn a corner and see a
pride of freaking lions advancing on you. 4. Now, imagine yourself as
a lion that has never been on a hunt. That has never walked outside
of a cage. That has been coddled and fed all of its life. And now your
world is exploding all around you. It's war, war, war. And then you
turn a corner and see a pride of freaking tanks advancing on you. 5. It's
okay to laugh. It's always okay to laugh at tragedy. If lions are capable
of laughter, then I'm positive those Baghdad lions were laughing at
their predicament. As they watched the city burn and collapse, I'm
sure a lioness turned to a lion and said, "So do you still think you're
the King of the Jungle?" 6. I don't know if the lions killed anybody
as they roamed through the streets. 7. But I'd guess they were too
afraid. I'm sure they could only see humans as zookeepers, not food.
8. In any case, the starving lions were eventually shot and killed by
U.S. soldiers on patrol. 9. It's a sad and terrible story, yes, but that
is war. And war is everywhere. And everywhere, there are prides of
starving lions wandering the streets. There are prides of starving lions
wandering inside your hearts. 10. You might also think that I'm using

starving lions as a metaphor for homeless folks, but I'm not. Homeless folks have been used far too often as targets for metaphors. I'm using those starving lions as a simple metaphor for hunger. All of our hunger. 11. Food-hunger. Love-hunger. Faith-hunger. Soul-hunger. 12. Who among us has not been hungry? Who among us has not been vulnerable? Who among us has not been a starving lion? Who among us has not been a prey animal? Who among us has not been a predator? 13. They say God created humans in God's image. But what if God also created lions in God's image? What if God created hunger in God's image? What if God is hunger? Tell me, how do you pray to hunger? How do you ask for hunger's blessing? How will hunger teach you to forgive? How will hunger teach you how to love? 14. Look out the window. It's all hunger and war. Hunger and war. Hunger and war. And the endless pride of lions.

from *Hanging Loose*

Control

◇　◇　◇

We are learning to control our thoughts,
to set obtrusive thoughts aside.

It takes an American
to do really big things.

Often I have no thoughts to push against.

It's lonely in a song
about outer space.

When I don't have any thoughts,
I want one!

A close-up reveals
that she has chosen

a plastic soap dish
in the shape of a giant sea turtle.

Can a thought truly be mine
if I am not currently thinking it?

There are two sides
to any argument;

one arm
in each sleeve.

★

Maybe I am always meditating,
if by that you mean

searching for a perfect
stranger.

from *A Public Space*

Breezeway

◊　◊　◊

Someone said we needed a breezeway
to bark down remnants of super storm Elias jugularly.
Alas it wasn't my call.
I didn't have a call or anything resembling one.
You see I have always been a rather dull-spirited winch.
The days go by and I go with them.
A breeze falls from a nearby tower
finds no breezeway, goes away
along a mission to supersize red shutters.

Alas if that were only all.
There's the children's belongings to be looked to
if only one can find the direction needed
and stuff like that.
I said we were all homers not homos
but my voice dwindled in the roar of Hurricane Edsel.
We have to live out our precise experimentation.
Otherwise there's no dying for anybody,
no crisp rewards.

Batman came out and clubbed me.
He never did get along with my view of the universe
except you know existential threads
from the time of the peace beaters and more.
He patted his dog Pastor Fido.
There was still so much to be learned
and even more to be researched.
It was like a goodbye. Why not accept it,
anyhow? The mission girls came through the woods

in their special suitings. It was all whipped cream and baklava.
Is there a Batman somewhere, who notices us
and promptly looks away, at a new catalog, say,
or another racing car expletive
coming back at Him?

from *The New Yorker*

ERIN BELIEU

With Birds

◇   ◇   ◇

It's all *Romeo and Juliet*—

hate crimes, booty calls, political
assassinations.

Who's more Tybalt than the Blue Jay?
More Mercutio than the mockingbird?

That ibis pretending to be a lawn ornament
makes a vain and stupid prince.

Birds living in their city-states, flinging
mob hits from the sky, they drop their dead

half chewed at my gates. But give anything

even one lice-riddled wing and suddenly
we're symbolic, in league with the adult

collector of teddy bears, the best-addressed-
in-therapy pinned like a kitty-cat calendar in

every cubicle. Pathetic, really. With birds,
make no exception.

                              Alright. It's possible
I'll give you this morning's

mourning doves, there on the telephone
wire, apart from the hoi polloi—

something in their pink, the exact shade
of an aubade. And shouldn't we recall

that keen pheromonal terror, when dawn
arrives too bright, too soon? Let's hope we

never muster what God put in the goose's
head. For this,
                                    you keep the doves.

from *The Normal School*

On Reflection

◇   ◇   ◇

—Michael Faraday

I will never contain the whole of it, he said,
the mirror too small for the long-necked lamp
floating swan-like near the angle of incidence.
Never, he said, stepping back from the lectern

and long-necked lamp, the mirror he held too small
for the swan. To reflect the object entirely,
he said, stepping back to the lectern,
the glass must be half the source's height.

To reflect the object entirely—the lamp,
or a swan, or my figure before you—
the glass must be half the source's height.
Unlike thought, which easily triples the whole.

My figure before you, the lamp's swan,
reflects my object entirely; that is, unlike
thought, which easily triples—or transforms—the whole,
the mirror is bound by harmony.

Entirely. Unlike the object reflected.
Finally, when you back away from the glass, your image—
the mirror is bound by harmony—
always doubles the distance between you.

As it finally backs away through the glass,
light doubling its loss through angles of reflection,

your image doubles the distance between you—always
twice as far from the source as you are before it:

Like a thought doubly lost through an act of reflection
floating swan-like past its angle of incidence,
twice as far from its mate as a lamp from a mirror
that will never contain the whole of it.

from *The Atlantic*

TRACI BRIMHALL

To Survive the Revolution

◊   ◊   ◊

I, too, love the devil. He comes to my bed
all wrath and blessing and wearing
my husband's beard, whispers, *tell me who
you suspect.* He fools me the same way every time,
but never punishes me the same way twice.
I don't remember who I give him but he says
I have the instinct for red. Kiss red. Pleasure red.
Red of the ripe guaraná, of the jaguar's eyes
when it stalks the village at night. Red as the child
I birthed who breathed twice and died.
The stump of flesh where the head should be,
red. Pierced side of Christ, red. A sinner needs
her sin, and mine is beloved. Mine returns
with skin under his fingernails, an ice cube
on his tongue, and covers my face with a hymnal.
I never ask for a miracle, only strength enough
to bear his weight. Each day, I hang laundry
on the line, dodge every shadow. Each night
he crawls through the window, I pay with a name.

from *The Kenyon Review*

Bird, Singing

◊   ◊   ◊

Then, every letter opened was an oyster
Of possible bad news, pried apart to reveal

The imperfect probable pearl of your death.

Then, urgent messages still affrighted me, sharp
Noises caused the birds not yet in flight to fly.

Then, this was the life of you.
All your molecules

Gathered for your dying off
Like mollusks clinging to a great ship's hull.

Ceremony of wounds, tinned,
Tiny swaddled starlings soaked in brine.

A bird, singing in his wicker cage, winds down.

Now, a trestle table lined with wooden platters
Neat with feathered wings of quail tucked-in.

Until you sever the thing, from self, it feels.
Thereafter it belongs to none.

You have nothing to be afraid of, anymore.

Outside Prague, I find you warm

Among the million small gold bees set loose
In April's onion snow, quietly

Quietly, would you sing this back to me, out loud?

from *Boston Review*

Host

◊   ◊   ◊

We want pictures of everything
Below your waist, and we want
Pictures of your waist. We can't
Talk right now, but we will text you
Into coitus. All thumbs. All bi-
Coastal and discreet and masculine
And muscular. No whites. Every
Body a top. We got a career
To think about. No face. We got
Kids to remember. No one over 29.
No one under 30. Our exes hurt us
Into hurting them. Disease free. No
Drugs. We like to get high with
The right person. You
Got a girl? Bring your boy.
We visiting. Room at the W.
Name's D. Name's J. We DeeJay.
We Trey. We Troy. We Q. We not
Sending a face. Where should we
Go tonight? You coming through? Please
Know what a gym looks like. Not much
Time. No strings. No place, no
Face. Be clean. We haven't met
Anyone here yet. Why is it so hard
To make friends? No games. You
Still coming through? Latinos only.
Blacks will do. We can take one right
Now. Text it to you. Be there next
Week. Be there in June. We not a phone

Person. We can host, but we won't meet
Without a recent pic and a real name
And the sound of your deepest voice.

from *Vinyl Poetry*

Pan del Muerto

◊   ◊   ◊

In Mexico, they bake bread
for those who died—flat
little cakes they leave around the house
for a mother or father or a child
to find. The dead are living
like us, growing fat, paying their debts,
brushing their teeth on schedule.
Sometimes it's hard to make your way
across a room to shake someone's
hand or give them a drink. The dead
are always there, in their evening gowns
and tuxedoes, expecting to be served—
asking for more crackers or champagne.
Just making love is a sacrilege!
The grandmother is there and the school
teacher and the delicate sister,
even those who are not yet born,
more innocent than babies. You get
up in the morning to comb your
hair and you are combing the brittle hair
of the dead, which goes on growing
like the eyelids and the finger
nails, as if the body were the last
to know or simply stubborn.
And maybe that's what the cakes are for—
to nourish the vanity of the corpse,
who after all would like to look
as good as possible on such a great
occasion. Listen! You hear the leaves

cracking faintly at dusk, a tire humming
on dry pavement, the sound of water
rushing through a pipe? The dead
are hungry! You must take
your knives and bowls and go down
into the cellar; you must begin to chant
those old recipes you've been saving—
mixing your own blood with the dry
sand the dead grow fat on,
that the children of the dead roll
into loaves for you to eat—
for the dust that will eventually pass
entirely through you.

from *Terminus Magazine*

wondering about our demise while driving to Disneyland with abandon

◊   ◊   ◊

don't be
afraid of
all we have pending
plasma I sold
in Albuquerque
broke even with
food I purchased to produce it
we can manage we can start under
this tree a quiet hour of
dozing into the bark will
reveal the step forward
things thinking about one another
this crystal and feather
ask me to bring them
together put them behind
the books they want a
private conversation and
that means me getting lost to
fellowship with grass soil and little
stones who tell me there is no clear
sense of when we leave this world
an owl drops a mouse in front of me
it doesn't have to mean something
but it probably does

help fishing a glass eye out of
the garbage disposal was my
favorite time helping anyone
he was so happy pushing it
back into his head shaking
my hand at the same time
we both wished he wasn't
my boyfriend's brother

from *Denver Quarterly*

A Fragment of Ibykos Translated 6 Ways

◊ ◊ ◊

[Ibykos fr. 286 *PMG*]
In spring, on the one hand,
the Kydonian apple trees,
being watered by streams of rivers
where the uncut garden of the maidens [is]
and vine blossoms
swelling
beneath shady vine branches
bloom.
On the other hand, for me
Eros lies quiet at no season.
Nay rather,
like a Thracian north wind
ablaze with lightning,
rushing from Aphrodite
accompanied by parching madnesses,
black,
unastonishable,
powerfully,
right up from the bottom of my feet
[it] shakes my whole breathing being.

[fr. 286 translated as "Woman's Constancy" by John Donne]
In woman, on the one hand,
those contracts
being purposed by change and falsehood,

20

where lovers' images [forswear the persons that we were],
and true deaths
sleeping
beneath true marriages,
antedate.
On the other hand, me
thy vow hast not conquered.
Nay rather,
like that new-made Tomorrow,
now disputing,
now abstaining,
accompanied by Love and his wrath,
truly,
not truly,
if I would,
if I could,
[it] justifies my one whole lunatic escape.

[fr. 286 as Bertolt Brecht's FBI file #100-67077]
At a cocktail party attended by known Communists, on the one hand,
the subject
being suitably paraphrased as Mr & Mrs Bert Brecht,
where ten years of exile have left their mark,
and beneath 5 copies of file 100-190707,
Charles Laughton
returning to the stage as Galileo,
enters an elevator.
On the other hand, of my name with a hyphen between Eugene and
Friedrich
the Bureau has no record.
Nay rather,
like the name of a certain Frenchman to whom Charles Laughton might send
packages,
accompanied by an unknown woman
who spoke to an unknown man,
or accompanied by an unknown man
who spoke to an unknown woman,
and in the event that all the captions are not correct,
please turn to page 307.

[fr. 286 as p. 47 of *Endgame* by Samuel Beckett]
In your kitchen, on the one hand,
bright corpses
starting to stink of having an idea,
where one of my legs [is]
and beneath sooner or later
the whole universe
doesn't ring and won't work.
On the other hand, I shouldn't think so.
Nay rather,
like a speck in the void,
pacing to and fro,
accompanied by the alarm,
frankly,
angrily,
impatiently,
not very convinced,
[it] kisses me goodbye. I'm dead. (Pause).

[Ibykos fr. 286 as pp. 136–37 of *Conversations with Kafka* by Gustav Janouch]
In the end, on the one hand, all those who sit behind us at the cash desks,
being engaged in the most destructive and hopeless rebellion there could
ever be,
where everything human [has been betrayed]
and
beneath the burden of existence
stock phrases,
with a gentle indefinable smile,
arouse suspicion.
On the other hand,
one who is afraid should not go into the wood.
Nay rather,
like modern armies,
accompanied by lightly spoken phrases in Czech or German,
fearlessly,
patiently,
unfortunately,
against myself,
against my own limitations and apathy,

against this very desk and chair I'm sitting in,
the charge is clear: one is condemned to life not death.

[fr. 286 as stops and signs from the London Underground]
At the excess fare window, on the one hand, the king's bakers,
ditching old shepherds for new elephants,
where east and west [cross north]
and beneath black friars forbidden from barking in church,
angels
mind the gap.
On the other hand,
a multi-ride ticket does not send me padding southwark.
Nay rather, like the seven sisters
gardening in the British Museum,
accompanied by penalties,
tooting,
turnpiked,
hackneyed,
Kentish,
cockfostered,
I am advised to expect delays all the way to the loo.

[fr. 286 as pp. 17–18 of *The Owner's Manual* of my new Emerson 1000W
microwave oven]
In hot snacks and appetizers, on the one hand, the soy, barbecue, Worcestershire
or steak sauce,
being sprinkled with paprika,
where a "browned appearance" [is desirable]
and beneath the magnetron tube
soggy crackers,
wrapped in bacon,
toughen.
On the other hand, a frozen pancake
will not crust.
Nay rather,
like radio waves,
bubbling,
spattering,
dispersing their spin,

and IMPORTANTLY should you omit to vent the plastic wrap,
or flip the pieces halfway through,
or properly position the special microwave popcorn popper,
[it] will burn your nose right off.

from *London Review of Books*

Hidden Bird

◊   ◊   ◊

Song birds enter the morning
the predawn before the fires,
you know, when the night floats away
like vapor on a lake,
or like kisses in the woods.
Songs that even creation
might not remember.

Continuous, threaded, as if
a cherry pit were stuck
in the throat
to produce the trumpet of the branches.
So varies, yet never, changing
through all the days, since
reptiles fell to earth.

I give up the reason for the sound
I give up the creature of sound
and the creator of the creatures
and of us and of dawn and
air and of vacuum
and human inhumanity.
I give up the song.
I give up the place.

from *The Nation*

HENRI COLE

City Horse

◊ ◊ ◊

At the end of the road from concept to corpse,
sucked out to sea and washed up again—
with uprooted trees, crumpled cars, and collapsed houses—
facedown in dirt, and tied to a telephone pole,
as if trying to raise herself still, though one leg is broken,
to look around at the grotesque unbelievable landscape,
the color around her eyes, nose, and mane (the dapples of roan,
a mix of white and red hairs) now powdery gray—
O, wondrous horse; O, delicate horse—dead, dead—
with a bridle still buckled around her cheeks—"She was more smarter than me,
she just wait," a boy sobs, clutching a hand to his mouth
and stroking the majestic rowing legs,
stiff now, that could not outrun
the heavy, black, frothing water.

from *The Threepenny Review*

The Helmet

◊　◊　◊

I spun the helmet on the ground and waited for it to stop. When it didn't stop, and probably two days had passed, I stood up and began snapping my fingers, just the one hand, my right hand, and I was kind of squatting a little, just bending my knees a bit, and tapping my right foot, and smiling I guess, like I was listening to something, something catchy. And after two more days of this, this finger-snapping, and after seeing that the helmet would continue to spin in the driveway, at this point I began to dance backward toward town, down the long dirt road toward the pavement that would take me to the highway that would eventually take me to town, always dancing and snapping, always moving backward, mile after mile, smiling, really getting down, never looking over my shoulder, falling and getting up, falling and getting up, traveling backward toward town, snapping, smiling, really covering some ground.

from *jubilat*

PHILIP DACEY

Juilliard Cento Sonnet

◊   ◊   ◊

At a Chamber Music Master Class

Use every centimeter of the hair.
That phrase needs elasticity, breathing room.
We need to hear the decoration more.
Her part has so many notes, it's almost a crime.

Tread lightly here—he's on his weakest string.
You can be perkier in the lower half of the bow.
Don't be so punctual; you're right but you're wrong.
Trios are three soloists. Soft doesn't mean slow.

Adjust your arm instead of the violin.
Attack, back off, and then attack again.
Let the sound of the chord decay before you go on.
When you have a rest, take it. You want your touch
to make the piano say, "Ah," not "Ouch."
Keep your hand rounded, as if it held a peach.

from *New Letters*

It Is to Have or Nothing

◊   ◊   ◊

Of all the forms of being—
I like a table
And
I like a lake.
The excitement of an upandcoming
Mistake:
Do not send word to your lover
If you cannot decide which one.
Involvement, like war, is a form
Of divination. Think
About what you said—or didn't—
That's why it hurts to swallow.
My first words in French?
Cruche, olivier, fenêtre.
Et, peut-être,
Pilier, tour.
Yeah, for a while they were "involved"—
Then they "delved" into
"Abjure."
Uncertainty more exciting than sex!
We could do serious, but
My lover was NO FUN.

O creamy cloud, indecision, I love you. I love you. I love you.
So badly. So slowly,
I want to enter you
From behind.
O ignorant protagonist
The lineaments of my face—

We had an interval,
A ludicrous,
"Us," the most fleeting
Of all.
I was
A tachiste, a revenant;
He a revanchist.
Yeah, what felt at what saw.
Listen: the next time you cry it won't be
At a train station
In France—you died at that scene—
To leave is to leave
Well enough.
I am so—
Not lonely.
Worn and dark was my . . .
Bright blue my . . .
Sometimes you just wanna press Send, thinking
If this is what ends it all, so I am.
I will send you Glück's purple bathing suit—
even if it kills us.
That's how I tell the story—"We were involved for a while—long was
Our distance—and, mostly—wrong—finally
I sent him Louise Glück's 'Purple Bathing Suit'—
Never to hear from him again."
The train schedule was an étude.
Was I no longer eager
To study my lover?
In my lap Coleridge's constancy to an ideal object.
In the end:
A newly cleared
Table.
And, if cleanly forgotten, a little lost
Lake.

from *Green Mountains Review*

News from Harlem

◊   ◊   ◊

for Marcus Mosiah Garvey

Even here on the south side of this city
of wind and blood, news is good for negroes.
A fat-faced, true African man, one of
those black men you know never ever
had a doubt that he is a man and strong,
too; one of those magic men
who know what God must feel like
standing over an army of angels; one
of those men who's stood at the edge
of the new century and seen a wide
world of what could be; a man who,
when he heard what Dubois said
about the color line thought right off
that this is going to be a century
where everybody will be talking
about niggers like they are new money,
and he, sure as hell, is going
to shine and shine. A man
with two big hands and a head
full of words who knows the freedom
of nothing to lose; a man who
knows the long legacy of rebels,
those maroons whispering Akan
in the hills—knife men, cutlass men,
roots men, Congo men;
those yellow-eyed quiet men
who look at death like it is

a good idea that someone came up
with; a man who learned by
touching the split chest of a white
man, his heart still thumping,
everything inside him slick
with blood and water, his ribs
pulled aside where the doctor
tried; that all white men
ain't nothing but flesh, old rotting
flesh like everybody else—
a man who's done the math
and knows that for fifty years,
his people have been waiting
for something bigger than themselves.
Well, news has it that this man
is causing trouble in Harlem
and the world won't be the same
when he's done with it. Even
here, the excitement of it is
rushing through the blues joints
and people are strutting about like
they have been marching, like
they been waving flags, like *they* shouting
the name of freedom beside
the round-faced black man,
with his proud high voice
showering imperatives on the folks
who gather to hear him talk
with his sweet island singing.
Black man sweating, dressed
clean with high collar and good
shoes. Yeah, this is good news
walking, cause we all need a daddy,
a man with a good firm voice,
a man who knows what we must
do to change this wearying world,
a man with a head full of dreams
of ships, seven miles of them
coming into that gaping Hudson
mouth, red, gold and green flags

flapping in the air—seven miles
of ships as far as the eye can see,
coming in, coming in, coming in.

from *Hayden's Ferry Review*

Elegy Indigo

◊   ◊   ◊

The text for today is early Miles, the Columbia years . . .
That tone pared down to essentials.

—Sekou Sundiata

"Did Miles mute his horn, because
a breeze can carry kites a gust might mutilate?"
Call him poet, professor. Call me shaky grasper of the chisel,
caught in a run-on rush to hammer it all.
The memory rushes in, frothing like a wave,
but recedes slowly as a blue crab across wet sand,
bright bits clasped in its claws.

Finally, finally, I come to believe in loss as a way of knowing.

How long does it take to hear what silence can say?
I stand at a stoplight, waiting for the colors to change.
At forty-five one has to deal with eyesight fading.
Not fading like blue from the knees of your favorite jeans
or lights on a stage above a silenced microphone,
but like a goateed poet in a stingy brim hat
covering the bets of a hooded man with holes for eyes
and scythes where his fingernails should be.

Finally, finally, I come to believe in loss as a way of knowing.

If the Blues is a river, doesn't it carry in and wash away?
LEDs are replacing halogen and incandescent lamps,
so the headlights of some approaching cars are slightly blue

as his velvet tone joins the voices of my fallen fathers.
And I tremble ever so softly, like a kite in a breeze
or the reed in a Harmon mute during a note's last linger.

Finally, finally . . . I come to believe in loss as a way of knowing.

from *Brilliant Corners*

These Hands, if Not Gods

◇　◇　◇

Haven't they moved like rivers—
like Glory, like light—
over the seven days of your body?

And wasn't that good?
Them at your hips—

isn't this what God felt when he pressed together
the first Beloved: *Everything.*
Fever. Vapor. Atman. Pulsus. Finally,
a sin worth hurting for. Finally, a sweet, a
You are mine.

It is hard not to have faith in this:
from the blue-brown clay of night
these two potters crushed and smoothed you
into being—grind, then curve—built your form up—

atlas of bone, fields of muscle,
one breast a fig tree, the other a nightingale,
both Morning and Evening.

O, the beautiful making they do—
of trigger and carve, suffering and stars—

Aren't they, too, the dark carpenters
of your small church? Have they not burned
on the altar of your belly, eaten the bread

of your thighs, broke you to wine, to ichor,
to nectareous feast?

Haven't they riveted your wrists, haven't they
had you at your knees?

And when these hands touched your throat,
showed you how to take the apple *and* the rib,
how to slip a thumb into your mouth and taste it all,
didn't you sing out their ninety-nine names—

Zahir, Aleph, Hands-time-seven,
Sphinx, Leonids, locomotura,
Rubidium, August, and September—
And when you cried out, *O, Prometheans,*
didn't they bring fire?

These hands, if not gods, then why
when you have come to me, and I have returned you
to that from which you came—bright mud, mineral-salt—
why then do you whisper, *O, my Hecatonchire. My Centimani.
My hundred-handed one?*

from *The Academy of American Poets Poem-a-Day*

Deep Lane

◇ ◇ ◇

Ned scrawls his self-delighted wild-boy trace
over the slopes of grass while I rest on a bench in the cemetery,
but we can't stay long,

it's a day I need to go into the city,
and when I stand up suddenly
my left leg's half a foot lower than my right,

because I've stepped into the sunken,
newly filled grave
of one Herbert Meyer. I don't know it then,

but that's when the wind blows up from beneath,

I think I'm just off balance, and make a joke of it later,
telling people my day began with falling into a grave,
and where can you go from there?

A few nights after
a storm blows down the moraine,
crisp and depth-charged with ozone and exhilaration,

chills my arms and face with that wind I've already met,
winds up the lanes and rattles the rose canes,
bends the beauty bush and Joe Pye weed down,

beautiful supplication,

the maple and walnut sway in the highest regions
of themselves, leaves circling in air
like the great curtain of bubbles blown by the humpback

to encircle the delicious schools—

Blows in my sleep
and blows while I'm cooking, blows while I read
and when I kiss does it ever blow then,
wind not particular to Mr. Meyer nor anyone else,
and thus the nervy thrill of its invitation: to be not at all

what you thought, unbound, to rush up

from the sinking earth on a gust of investigation:
now go be the crooked little house,
and the cracks in the shingles,

tunnel your hour as the mouse in the stale loaf,

fly back to the strong hands of the baker,
flour powdering a happy shroud
around the coursing veins in his forearms.

Spring backward into the wheat,
forward into the belly of the mouse-child

—what reason to ever end?

Well I know one:
if you don't hold still, you can have joy after joy,

but you can't stay anywhere to love.
That's the price, that rib-rattling wind
waiting to sweep you up,

that's the price the wind pays.

from *Ploughshares*

The Blues Is a Verb

◇ ◇ ◇

Pray without speech. Bear witness walking
and dying slowly. In the whole universe
this one and only place which you have
made your very own. An instant of provocation
without the proper greeting. And down 6th street,
car alarms ululating. A fifth is your morning
medicine. A silhouette in chalk
on the sidewalk watches the children
run. Down and up Second Avenue
a red Monte Carlo, slows in an
old shark-skinned suit, the air
like furious birds. Someone leans against the brick wall
sharing a cigarette, blue-black under the fire escape.
Mrs. Janofsky's boy nods into his own hands.
The poor are many and so the women come
and go, bruises on their eyes like fake sapphires.
Men who never not hear the noise in their heads.
But not knowing the dead, roaming the streets
like feral cats, you hurl yourself into the oncoming traffic
of their eyes. Somewhere a search has been called off.
Whitecaps cover your mouth as you struggle
not to drown. You stick your fucking finger
in the socket. You cannot holler.
All the street assassins know you can break
a man's neck in a second flat; they grin
at their electronic palms. They enter and exit
through broken arteries. A razor left by the mirror.
The ghost lines of cocaine and tar,

along the boulevard beneath the diseased
elms. Someone wishes a lottery ticket with a nickel.

from *Spillway*

The Spring Cricket Repudiates His Parable of Negritude

◊   ◊   ◊

Hell,

we just climbed. Reached the lip
and fell back, slipped

and started up again—
climbed to be climbing, sang

to be singing. It's just what we do.
No one bothered to analyze our blues

until everybody involved
was strung out or dead; to solve

everything that was happening
while it was happening

would have taken some serious opium.
Seriously: All wisdom

is afterthought, a sort of helpless relief.
So don't go thinking none of this grief

belongs to you: Even if
you don't know how it

feels to fall, you can get my drift;
and I, who live it

daily, have heard
that perfect word

enough to know just when
to use it—as in:

Oh hell. Hell, no.
No—

this is hell.

from *Poet Lore*

CAMILLE DUNGY

Conspiracy
(to breathe together)

◊　◊　◊

Last week, a woman smiled at my daughter and I wondered
if she might have been the sort of girl my mother says spat on my aunt
when they were children in Virginia all those acts and laws ago.

Half the time I can't tell my experiences apart from the ghosts'.

A shirt my mother gave me settles into my chest.

I should say *onto my chest*, but I am self-conscious—
the way the men watch me while I move toward them
makes my heart trip and slide and threaten to bruise
so that, inside my chest, I feel the pressure of her body,
her mother's breasts, her mother's mother's big, loving bounty.

I wear my daughter the way women other places are taught
to wear their young. Sometimes, when people smile,
I wonder if they think I am being quaintly primitive.

The cloth I wrap her in is brightly patterned, African,
and the baby's hair manes her alert head in such a way
she has often been compared to an animal.

There is a stroller in the garage, but I don't want to be taken
as my own child's nanny. (Half the time I know my fears are mine alone.)

At my shower, a Cameroonian woman helped me practice
putting a toy baby on my back. I stood in the middle of a circle
of women, stooped over and fumbling with the cloth. Curious George
was the only doll on hand, so the white women looked away
afraid I would hurt my baby while the black women looked away
and thought about not thinking about monkeys.

There is so much time in the world. How many ways can it be divided?

I walk every day with my daughter and wonder
what is happening in other people's minds. Half the time
I am filled with terror. Half the time I am full of myself.

The baby is sleeping on my back again. When I stand still,
I can feel her breathing. But when I start to move, I lose her
in the rhythms of my tread.

from *The American Poetry Review*

Overturned

◇ ◇ ◇

What did you hear
That got you talking raw?
You got that low cloud look,
Got that heart-nicked stare.

Like the flora got voted
From under your feet.
Like someone told you a story,

Maybe the wrong story,
Palm trees where there should
Be pine. And now you doubt

Everything. Don't you hate
Doubting everything? There's
An unease the body radiates

When it can't put a finger
On a lie. You got that pickle
Wince, my friend,

You look like
You lost the directions
To where you from.

from *Terminus Magazine*

Fallen

◊　◊　◊

But I was never the light of my father's eyes, nor any
well-lit brother's (that deep-husked choir), so there
was no height from which to fall. I began here
                    in the proverbial bottom:
undertow, base from which one may rise but briefly,
like the failing horse knowing it must now race, must
tear out of its rusted gate, must further tear
the pleurisied lining of its lungs, let its tongue loll
                    ugly from the side
of its mouth. Have you seen such a thing?
Its brown coat salted with sweat as it lunges
forward and lunges again, forcing its measure
not up but out, knowing its ankles could fold
under such weight, its nose opened
into another being, sucking and snorting
the only thing it takes within that does not judge it,
the air. The sweet, sweet air
as it makes its way around a curve that might kill it,
that assuredly will kill it. Do you see me there?
Of course not.
                    I'm over here. Here,
in *this* hollow running for my low life. O Father,
for the rub of a hand over my back. O Brothers,
for the gold leaf wreath that might have meant
a stroke of my calf, for that, I stretch these legs to breaking,
I wrench this belly's hull, dark
as all alluvial things are. Lucifer's is a common story, a
child's bogeyman. What should frighten *you* is this:
Imagine what he would be had he not fallen, had he never

known the elusive light at all, *never* been privy to the cords
of God's neck, if he in fact doubted such things,
believing only in what anguishes and writhes, trusting
nothing more than what soils his hands.

from *Prairie Schooner*

To the Fig Tree
on 9th and Christian

◊   ◊   ◊

Tumbling through the
city in my
mind without once
looking up
the racket in
the lugwork probably
rehearsing some
stupid thing I
said or did
some crime or
other the city they
say is a lonely
place until yes
the sound of sweeping
and a woman
yes with a
broom beneath
which you are now
too the canopy
of a fig its
arms pulling the
September sun to it
and she
has a hose too
and so works hard
rinsing and scrubbing
the walk

lest some poor sod
slip on the
silk of a fig
and break his hip
and not probably
reach over to gobble up
the perpetrator
the light catches
the veins in her hands
when I ask about
the tree they
flutter in the air and
she says take
as much as
you can
help me
so I load my
pockets and mouth
and she points
to the stepladder against
the wall to
mean more but
I was without a
sack so my meager
plunder would have to
suffice and an old woman
whom gravity
was pulling into
the earth loosed one
from a low slung
branch and its eye
wept like hers
which she dabbed
with a kerchief as she
cleaved the fig with
what remained of her
teeth and soon there were
eight or nine
people gathered beneath
the tree looking into

it like a
constellation pointing
do you see it
and I am tall and so
good for these things
and a bald man even
told me so
when I grabbed three
or four for
him reaching into the
giddy throngs of
yellow jackets sugar
stoned which he only
pointed to smiling and
rubbing his stomach
I mean he was really rubbing his stomach
like there was a baby
in there
it was hot his
head shone while he
offered recipes to the
group using words which
I couldn't understand and besides
I was a little
tipsy on the dance
of the velvety heart rolling
in my mouth
pulling me down and
down into the
oldest countries of my
body where I ate my first fig
from the hand of a man who escaped his country
by swimming through the night
and maybe
never said more than
five words to me
at once but gave me
figs and a man on his way
to work hops twice
to reach at last his

fig which he smiles at and calls
baby, *c'mere baby,*
he says and blows a kiss
to the tree which everyone knows
cannot grow this far north
being Mediterranean
and favoring the rocky, sun-baked soils
of Jordan and Sicily
but no one told the fig tree
or the immigrants
there is a way
the fig tree grows
in groves it wants,
it seems, to hold us,
yes I am anthropomorphizing
goddammit I have twice
in the last thirty seconds
rubbed my sweaty
forearm into someone else's
sweaty shoulder
gleeful eating out of each other's hands
on Christian St.
in Philadelphia a city like most
which has murdered its own
people
this is true
we are feeding each other
from a tree
at the corner of Christian and 9th
strangers maybe
never again.

from *The American Poetry Review*

Liner Notes for Monk

◇   ◇   ◇

"Monk's Mood" [false start]

I had gotten off the bus too soon for my stop and so I had to walk a few
blocks in order to gain my bearings. Thelonious Monk said, "It's always night/ or
we
wouldn't need light." I read this in an essay. I wanted to have a conversation
with someone to lighten my load. I remember seeing a woman disembarking
from the next
bus. Our gazes locked for a long second. [*It is always night wherever you go.*]

"Crepuscule with Nellie" [breakdown]

[*Monk continues alone and quiet.*] Northward leads to the river southward back to
my hotel
room. An entire week had gone by and I hadn't exchanged seven words with
another
human. The sound of words directed at me would feel like a hand on my
shoulder, an arm
brushing against my skin. It is always night when silence overcomes me, silence
opening up
within me like a wound. Black keys, I've been told, have an ominous, mysterious
sound.

"Misterioso"

[*Monk conversing with water.*] What we end up making, whether it's something we
     do by
ourselves or with others is always a form of conversation. My presence is solid,
     but
others see me as a fishing weir, a foamless Mister So-
and-So, a scavenger for anything that would flatter his eyes. What I want is a
     garden that will not perish, a bed of imperial, white peonies.

from *Tongue*

One El Paso, Two El Paso

◊   ◊   ◊

Awake in the desert to the sound of calling.
Must be the mountain, I thought.

The violent border, I assumed, though the boundary
line between the living and the dead was erased years ago.

Awake in the sand, I feared, old shoes decorated with
razor wire, a heaven of light on the peaks.

Must be time to get up, I assumed. Parked outside,
Border Patrol vehicles, I had to choose.

Awake to follow immigration shadows vanishing inside
American walls, river drownings counted as they cross,

Maria Salinas's body dragged out, her mud costume
pasted with plastic bottles and crushed beer cans,

black water flowing to bless her in her sleep.
Must be the roar of illegal death, I decided,

a way out of the current, though satellite maps never
show the brown veins of the concrete channel.

Awake in the arroyo of a mushroom cloud, I choke,
1945 explosion in the sand, eternal radioactive wind,

the end of one war mutating the border into another
that also requires fatal skills of young men because few

dream the atomic bomb gave birth in La Jornada,
historic trail behind the mountain realigned, then cut

off from El Paso, the town surrounded with barbed
wire, the new century kissing car bombs, drug cartels,

massacres across the river, hundreds shot in ambushes
and neighborhood soccer games that always score.

Wake up, I thought, look south to the last cathedral
in Juarez before its exploding bricks hurtle this way.

Make the sign of the cross, open your eyes to one town,
two cities, five centuries of praying in the beautiful dust.

from *Barrow Street*

The River Twice

◇   ◇   ◇

The Love of Jesus is a thrift warehouse on the south side of town. Everything

nside is a dollar. On Mondays & Fridays, everything is fifty cents.
A stormy afternoon in June & I drift for hours down the aisles: bread machines

& coffee pots. Shirts
               & shoes. Teetering stacks of mismatched dinnerware.

am studying a cup whose crackled glaze is the pale blue-green of beach glass.
Two lions chase one another around its fragile eternity,

he way the lover pursues the beloved on the ancient urn, their manes & legs

washed in a preternatural purple & gold.
                       Behind me, a woman tells her son William
o get up from the floor so that she can measure him against a pair

of little boys' jeans. When he doesn't rise, she tells him she is going to start

ounting. She says she is only going to count to two.
                     When I look over,
ae is already on his feet at silent attention, his arms outstretched from his sides.

live in an attic apartment above two women who have been unemployed

s long as I have known them.
                   This week the last of their benefits
aas been unexpectedly terminated by the state.
                     A drop in the overall number

of jobless automatically triggers the cessation of extensions, the letter

that comes in the mail explains.
Outside, thunder cracks. Later, the streets
will be full of limbs.
Heraclitus believed that in the beginning

creation simply bubbled forth, an inevitable percolating stream—*logos*,

both reason & word—issuing from a source unseen. Sometimes
I feel a sudden sorrow, as though my own emotions were a room
I'd forgotten why I entered.
My mother struck me only once—

for refusing to put on my coat. I was four years old & she had been scrubbing
motel rooms all day.
I'd fallen asleep in the dark on a low shelf

in the linen closet beside the boxes of little pink soaps.
Today, that shelf

is gone & the great white polar caps
are melting. At Kasungu National Park
in Malawi, a drought has caused the lions to turn on the rangers

whose job it is to protect them.
Our skulls are chipped bowls, broken

globes, we plunge into the flow.
Heraclitus, whom the crash of time has left
in fragments, saw in the cosmos a harmony of tensions.
Imagine

the lyre, he wrote, & the bow. The store radio plays satellite gospel.

A hymn with the chorus *Every moment you shall be judged* is followed
by one in which the choir shouts *Praise! Stand up and be forgiven.*

from *Painted Bride Quarterly*

SCRIPT POEM

◇ ◇ ◇

INT. APARTMENT/LIVING ROOM—DAY

SHE brushes her teeth next to the coffee table. The CAT sighs in the armchair. A CROW unseen cries outside the window.

CROW (V.O.)
Caw, caw, caw, caw.

EXT. MAILBOX—DAY

The MAILMAN hands her a brown package.

MAILMAN
It's heavy.

SHE
I got it.

The mailman just came back from fighting in Iraq.
His large blue body hovers in the fog.

MAILMAN
Are you going away this weekend?

SHE
No.

Lightning bolts out of his eyes.

MAILMAN
It's a holiday.

SHE
I know.

She looks away.
Sand pours out of her heart.

EXT. BUS STOP—DAY

She eats an apple.

INT. APARTMENT/BATHROOM—NIGHT

Pink and white tiles on the floor. She flosses.

SHE
                    (whispers)
I didn't mean to shoot him at the temple.

Black wings flap and enfold her heart.

EXT. MAILBOX—NIGHT

The wind blows.

from *MAKE*

As Like

◇   ◇   ◇

In times of the most extreme potatoes
My hair is very thin,
Almost ink-like.
Space is like an accordion,
Accordion-like.
But also, our fingers become accordions
And start dancing.

In times of the most extreme bossa nova
Your pants are very thin,
Almost transparent.
Space is very interesting to think about
But so are your pants.
But also, the wind is very cold
And we freeze, like accordions.

In times of the most extreme minnows
The windows are very dark,
Almost intransigent.
Water is harmonica-perforated;
The fish, of course, go back and forth.
But also, the little boats turn around
And around in the sink, like accordions.

In times of the most extreme unction
My name is very thin,
Almost zipper-like.
Space is very thin also;
And distance is that way too.

But also, the stars become very accordion-like
So we eat them.

In times of the most extremely long, emotional, blue lines
The rest of the lines
Get very thin,
Almost meaningless.
Vegetables arise out of nowhere and change.
But also, the letter V becomes invisible
And unpronounceable.

from *Pleiades*

Blue prints

◊   ◊   ◊

Up and up the mountain, but suddenly a flat spot
exactly the size of the house they would build,
and when they went to dig for the foundation, the foundation
appeared, just as the beams for the floor, as they started
to set them in place, revealed they had always been there,

it was like coming into the room to find your diary
writing itself, she told the interviewer, who wanted to talk
about her paintings but she kept coming back to the house,
including the sky above the house, how it resembled
her childhood, forgetting how to rain
when it wasn't raining, remembering blue
just when she needed to be startled most, don't you think

it odd that my life has always had just enough space
for my life, she asked the man's recorder
as much as the man, hoping the recorder
would consider the question and get back to her, then you moved
to Madrid, the interviewer was saying, and started painting
your invisible landscapes, I remember the first window

we lifted into place, she replied, that the view of the valley
it would hold was already in the glass when we cut the cardboard box
away, we just lined them up, the premonition
with the day, he had twenty more questions

but crossed them off, I have always wanted to build a room
around a painting, he said, yes, she replied, a painting
hanging in space, he added, a painting of a woman

adjusting a wall to suit a painting, she said, like how the universe
began, he suggested, did it begin, she wondered, is that
what this is?

from *The Believer*

No Doubt About It
(I Gotta Get Another Hat)

◊   ◊   ◊

after Chris Toll

in my head it was Vincent (not Boris)
who narrated the Who family fun
during Grinch-time in December
but then he clocked in for Sears
selling Rembrandts (not Lady Kenmores)
(clarity at 14)
why is *he*
in *crèche*

I met Santa
(who fingered a pocketful of poems)
on the corner of Saint Paul + No(wH)ere
four times maybe three
he passed out couplets to the crowd
a smile full of antlers
(Bullwinkle not Rudolph)
I know why *Chris*
            is in *Christmas*

some gods play with clouds
like Play-Doh
(who forgot to wind the clock)
some poets cloud with play
like heart tracings

why is *toll*
        in *atoll*

how does a poet
fall back into the sky
(what time is it)
I'm sure certain only twice each day
this is once
I know why *he*
        is in *ache*

from *Little Patuxent Review*

Write Whiter

◊ ◊ ◊

Obviously, it's a category I've been made aware of
                                    from time to time.
It's been pointed out that my characters eat a lot of lightly-braised asparagus
and get FedEx packages almost daily.

Yet I *dislike* being thought of as a white writer.
I never wanted to be limited like that.

When I find my books in the "White Literature" section of the bookstore,
                              dismay is what I feel—
I thought I was writing about other, larger things.

Tax refunds, Spanish lessons, premature ejaculation;
meatloaf and sitcoms; the fear of perishing.

I know some readers need to see their lives reflected from the page—
It lets them know they aren't alone.

The art it takes to make that kind of comfort
                    is not something I look upon with scorn.

But after a while, you start to feel like, to the world, white
                                    is all you'll ever be.

And gradually, after all the struggling against,
after tasting your own fear of being

only what you are,
you accept—

Then, with fresh determination, you lean forward again.
You write whiter and whiter.

from *The Paris Review*

OK Cupid

◇　◇　◇

Dating a Catholic is like dating a tribe
    and dating a tribe is like dating a nation
and dating a nation is like dating a football star
    and dating a football star is like dating a new car
and dating a new car is like dating an air freshener
    and dating an air freshener is like dating a fake tree
and dating a fake tree is like dating silver tinsel
    and dating silver tinsel is like dating a holiday
and dating a holiday is like dating a black man
    and dating a black man is like dating a top
and dating a top is like dating a bottom
    and dating a bottom is like dating a Tibetan
and dating a Tibetan is like dating a dragon
    and dating a dragon is like dating a fireplace
and dating a fireplace is like dating a mantel
    and dating a mantel is like dating a picture frame
and dating a picture frame is like dating Martin Luther King with Jesus
    and dating Martin Luther King & Jesus is like dating a threesome
and dating a threesome is like dating a commune
    and dating a commune is like dating an unachievable idea
and dating an idea is like dating the Enlightenment
    and dating the Enlightenment is like dating science
and dating science is like dating a beaker
    and dating a beaker is like dating a pharmacy
and dating a pharmacy is like dating a dealer
    and dating a dealer is like dating a supply chain
and dating a supply chain is like dating a Republican
    and dating a Republican is like dating winter

and dating winter is like dating Demeter
  and dating Demeter is like dating corn
and dating corn is like dating pancakes
  and dating pancakes is like dating an orgasm
and dating an orgasm is like dating Utopia
  and dating Utopia is like dating an Amish woman
and dating an Amish woman is like dating a Luddite
  and dating a Luddite is like dating a folk hero
and dating a folk hero is like dating Robert Zimmerman
  and dating Robert Zimmerman is like dating history
and dating history is like dating a white man
  and dating a white man is like dating insecurity
and dating insecurity is like dating a Hummer
  and dating a Hummer is like dating The Pentagon
and dating The Pentagon is like dating a lost star
  and dating a lost star is like dating a liberal
and dating a liberal is like dating a Jew
  and dating a Jew is like dating a lamp
and dating a lamp is like dating a blonde
  and dating a blonde is like dating a Swede
and dating a Swede is like dating IKEA
  and dating IKEA is like dating Whole Foods
and dating Whole Foods is like dating a yoga instructor
  and dating a yoga instructor is like dating an e-reader
and dating an e-reader is like dating a television
  and dating a television is like dating a commercial
and dating a commercial is like dating a serial murderer
  and dating a serial murderer is like dating Raskolnikov
and dating Raskolnikov is like dating a rationalist
  and dating a rationalist is like dating an academic
and dating an academic is like dating a CV
  and dating a CV is like dating a white woman
and dating a white woman is like dating a bread line
  and dating a bread line is like dating a refugee
and dating a refugee is like dating a Cuban
  and dating a Cuban is like dating a propane flame
and dating a flame is like dating a topless jihadist
  and dating a jihadist is like dating a femme fatale
and dating a femme fatale is like dating Paris Hilton
  and dating Paris Hilton is like dating a tabloid

and dating a tabloid is like dating a Communist
    and dating a Communist is like dating cut flowers
and dating cut flowers is like dating infidelity
    and dating infidelity is like dating a pool

from *Tin House*

L.A. Police Chief Daryl Gates Dead at 83

◊   ◊   ◊

—We were the finest.

So the parents blamed the children,
and the children marched barefoot
through the alleys, spray-painting
their age. And the preacher introduced
the word "lascivious" and accused
the congregation of not tiding
when the daughter died.
And the deacon board smoked.
And the economists saluted Reagan.
And the police called it an economy of dust.
Our meteorologist predicted
a low-pressure system in the abdomen.
And the junkies swore perfume rung the air.
The grocer had his union; the butcher couldn't
outrun his quarter of spoiled blood.
And the girls wore extra rings
and caked their skin with Vaseline.
And the men slept the afternoon,
growing childishly morose as they dreamed.
And I think I thought we'd burn then,
when the refinery blew, and rust began
to bleed through the whitewashed fence,

when the lawns were done, and the schoolyard
darkened, and the side streets began to split.

from *Crazyhorse*

The Labor of
Stagger Lee: Boar

◊   ◊   ◊

pigs prey to piggishnesses. get ate from the rooter to the tooter.
I'm a hog for you baby, I can't get enough go the wolfish crooner.
the gust buffeted porker roll in the hay or laid down
      in twig rapine. let me in, let me in.

        no drum-gut, Stagger's stomach a tenement:
his deadeye bigger than his brick house.
Stagger Lee live by the want and die by the noose,
whose greedy void like a whorehouse
      full of empties getting full. can't get enough!
rumored Stagger would root through pussy
to plumb a fat boy. here piggy! what Lee see he seize.
manful, ham-fisted. sorry Billy,
      your name mud and who love dirt like swine?
they get in it like a straw house. it'll be cold out
before Lee admit his squeals weren't howls.
he got down. he get dirty.

from *Poetry*

Negritude

◊   ◊   ◊

I have also been left singing "Careless Love"
   but my negritude is nobody's coonskin cap
on a mountaintop or down by the riverside.

My negritude has sucked all the joy juice
   from the days of wild virginal forests
I made to kneel with axe & crosscut.

My negritude has beaten tom-toms
   till the drawstring of doubt unraveled
& blood leaked on my blue suede shoes.

My negritude came a long ways to find me
   in Louisiana beside beckoning quicksand,
a disappearing act & the double limbo.

My negritude is the caul worked into soil
   brought back to life by cosmic desire
& gratitude baked into my daily bread.

My negritude sways before a viper's
   truth serum on an iron spearhead,
belladonna tucked behind my left ear.

From afar, Cesaire, your wit & fidelity
   made me stumble-dance a half mile
here, beyond any puppet's hallelujah,

while Grandmama sat in a wheelchair
   among the tangled rows of collards,
okra, speckled peas, & sweet corn,

digging with a hoe honed so many years
   the blade was a quarter moon—all the
strength she had in her twisted body.

Now, even if this is a sign of my negritude,
   I still remember a rain-drenched sun
rising out of the loony old scrub oaks.

Sure, I know the tiger neither speaks
   of her tigritude nor the blood she's left
on grass & wildflowers around the tombs.

from *Gris-Gris*

HAILEY LEITHAUSER

In My Last Past Life

◊   ◊   ◊

In my last past life I had a nut brown wife,
a gray and white house looking over the sea,
a forest for love and a river for grief,

a lantern for hope, for courage a knife,
a city for distance, lights spread on the sea.
In my last past life I had a brown wife

subtle and busy and contented and brief,
(she stood in the dusk silhouette with the sea)
a forest and love and a river, and grief

was a ghost hidden green in the leaves,
an echo off cliffs that bound back the sea.
In that life it would last, my past and my wife,

the wren in the garden, the moon on the roof,
the day winds that flirted and teased at the sea,
the forest that loved and the river that grieved

the life that was garden and day wind and thief
(each sunrise and sundown the turn of the sea)
the life that I had, and my last brown wife,
a forest for love, a still river for grief.

from *Southwest Review*

Elegy with a Darkening Trapeze inside It

◇   ◇   ◇

The idea turned out to be no more than a cart wheel
Stuck in mud, & unturned fields spreading to the horizon while
Two guys in a tavern went on drinking *tsuica* & recalling their one

Accomplishment in life—the seduction of a virgin on the blank
Pedestal of a statue where Stalin had once stood.

The State is an old man's withered arm.

~

The only surviving son of Jesus Christ was Karl Marx.
You can tell by the last letter of his name,
Which has the shape & frail balance of an overturned cross

On a windswept hillside. It marked the end of things.
Of lumber that rots & falls. The czar is a shattered teacup,

The trouble with a good idea is that it has to work:

The only surviving son of Jesus Christ survives now
Mostly in English departments & untended graves.

One thing he said I still remember, a thing that's never there
When I try to look it up, was: "Sex should be no more important . . .
Than a glass of water." It sounded vaguely like the kind of thing

Christ might have said if Christ had a sense of humor.
The empty bar that someone was supposed to swing to him
Did not arrive, & so his outstretched flesh itself became

A darkening trapeze. The two other acrobats were thieves.

~

My colleague Otto Fick, who twenty years ago
Wrote brilliant lectures on the air, sometimes
Would pause & seem to consult notes left
On a podium, & then resume. A student once
Went up after class to look at them & found
Only a blank sheet of paper. Nothing there.
"In theory, I believe in Marx. In fact, my wife
Has to go in next week for another
Biopsy. Fact is disbelief. One day it swells up
In front of you, the sky, the sunlight on everything,

Traffic, kids on surfboards waiting for the next
Big set off San Onofre. It's all still there . . . just
There for someone else, not for you." This is what
My friend Otto told me as we drove to work.

~

I worked with men in vineyards once who were paid
In wages thin as water, cash that evaporated & rose like heat.
They lived in rows of makeshift sheds the owner hauled

Into an orchard too old to bother picking anymore,
And where, at dusk, a visible rushing hunger

Raced along the limbs of the trees surrounding them.
Their kids would watch it happen until a whole tree would seem
To vanish under it. There were so many of them.

By then the rats were flying over a sickening trapeze of leaves
And the tree would darken suddenly. It would look like brown water

Rushing silently & spreading everywhere

Before it got dark anyway & the kids went in.
"There was more rats in there than there was beads on all the rosaries of the dead.
We wen' to confession all the time then 'cause we thought we might disappear

Under them trees. There was a bruja in the camp but we dint go to her no more.
She couldn't predict nothing. And she'd always cry when you asked her questions,"

A woman said who had stayed there for a while.

Every revolution ends, or it begins, in memory:
Someone remembering her diminishment & pain, the way
Her scuffed shoes looked in the pale light,
How she inhaled steel filings in the grinding shed
For thirty years without complaining once about it,
How she might have done things differently. But didn't.
How it is too late to change things now. How it isn't.

from *Blackbird*

Sermon of the Dreadnaught

◊   ◊   ◊

The guitar: I take communion
daily in this shack of a church
with a moaner's bench rubbed
smooth by repentant backsliders.
I listen to the seventh note,
graced by God, it is my battle-axe,
a joyful noise no more modern
than that old-time religion
cooking on the woodstove
in my grandmothers' kitchens.
Holy ghosted, I have been washed
in the blackwater cypress swamp
that flows inside my guitar.
A solid top, and I play it righteous
as any stingy brim disciple that ever
has played a small town bus stop,
and I got a missing canine tooth
from the right side of my mouth
and now my gospel is cobalt blue.
I remember the purity of the old guys,
Lucky Strike smokers and homebrew
drinkers with open tunings, sanctified
imperfections, scarred and battered
harmonies. They have introduced me
to the hollering haints who now hold
late night prayer service in my guitar.
I believe in the palm oil that anoints
the guitar. I believe in life as sure
as I believe in death. I confess

the ancestor spirits and their love
accompanies me. The bloodline
has dressed me in that glorious suit
that we only wear when we are
our true selves. In the ascending heat
there is a train of guitar moments,
boxcars of dualities in the everyday
choices that we make. I have been
delivered, blessed by this guitar
that brought me home from forty years
in the urban American deserts,
back to the piney woods of Carolina,
this old rugged guitar, my cross
to bear, this everlasting church
of the mule-driving sharecroppers.

from *MiPOesias*

Elegy for My Mother

◇　◇　◇

But I still have my river-mother
and all of her glittering fish,

my sycamore-mother who never is cold,

my star-white mother whose eyes
need no closing,

whose wind-stripped hands need not crochet,

whose dove-plain dress does not rip
on the drag of the gutter's wind,

whose kicked-off galoshes never lined up
with all the black pumps of the mothers
of Hillcrest Road,

my mother whose fiddle has two
curved hurts for its f-holes,

magnolia-mother shedding her petals of snow,
tearless November mother refusing soup,

leaving her wig on the steps
for the grackles to nest in,

my broad-boned mother, my corduroy
notre dame of worn knees,

mother of sidestroke stillness
and loose knots,

my mother who blurs from the effort
of being remembered,

O homely, deliberate icon of lamps left on,

and I have set out a dish for her fingerbeams

from *FIELD*

Rape Joke

◇ ◇ ◇

The rape joke is that you were 19 years old.

The rape joke is that he was your boyfriend.

The rape joke it wore a goatee. A goatee.

Imagine the rape joke looking in the mirror, perfectly reflecting back itself, and grooming itself to look more like a rape joke. "Ahhhh," it thinks. "Yes. *A goatee.*"

No offense.

The rape joke is that he was seven years older. The rape joke is that you had known him for years, since you were too young to be interesting to him. You liked that use of the word "interesting," as if you were a piece of knowledge that someone could be desperate to acquire, to assimilate, and to spit back out in different form through his goateed mouth.

Then suddenly you were older, but not very old at all.

The rape joke is that you had been drinking wine coolers. Wine coolers! Who drinks wine coolers? People who get raped, according to the rape joke.

The rape joke is he was a bouncer, and kept people out for a living.

Not you!

The rape joke is that he carried a knife, and would show it to you, and would turn it over and over in his hands as if it were a book.

He wasn't threatening you, you understood. He just really liked his knife.

The rape joke is he once almost murdered a dude by throwing him through a plate-glass window. The next day he told you and he was trembling, which you took as evidence of his sensitivity.

How can a piece of knowledge be stupid? But of course you were so stupid.

The rape joke is that sometimes he would tell you you were going on a date and then take you over to his best friend Peewee's house and make you watch wrestling while they all got high.

The rape joke is that his best friend was named Peewee.

OK, the rape joke is that he worshipped The Rock.

Like the dude was completely in love with The Rock. He thought it was so great what he could do with his eyebrow.

The rape joke is he called wrestling "a soap opera for men." Men love drama too, he assured you.

The rape joke is that his bookshelf was just a row of paperbacks about serial killers. You mistook this for an interest in history, and laboring under this misapprehension you once gave him a copy of Günter Grass's *My Century*, which he never even tried to read.

It gets funnier.

The rape joke is that he kept a diary. I wonder if he wrote about the rape in it.

The rape joke is that you read it once, and he talked about another girl. He called her Miss Geography, and said "he didn't have those urges when he looked at her anymore," not since he met you. Close call, Miss Geography!

The rape joke is that he was your father's high school student—your father taught World Religion. You helped him clean out his classroom at the end of the year, and he let you take home the most beat-up textbooks.

The rape joke is that he knew you when you were twelve years old. He once helped your family move two states over, and you drove from Cincinnati to St. Louis with him, all by yourselves, and he was kind to you, and you talked the whole way. He had chaw in his mouth the entire time, and you told him he was disgusting and he laughed, and spat the juice through his goatee into a Mountain Dew bottle.

The rape joke is that *come on*, you should have seen it coming. This rape joke is practically writing itself.

The rape joke is that you were facedown. The rape joke is you were wearing a pretty green necklace that your sister had made for you. Later you cut that necklace up. The mattress felt a specific way, and your mouth felt a specific way open against it, as if you were speaking, but you know you were not. As if your mouth were open ten years into the future, reciting a poem called Rape Joke.

The rape joke is that time is different, becomes more horrible and more habitable, and accommodates your need to go deeper into it.

Just like the body, which more than a concrete form is a capacity.

You know the body of time is *elastic*, can take almost anything you give it, and heals quickly.

The rape joke is that of course there was blood, which in human beings is so close to the surface.

The rape joke is you went home like nothing happened, and laughed about it the next day and the day after that, and when you told people you laughed, and that was the rape joke.

It was a year before you told your parents, because he was like a son to them. The rape joke is that when you told your father, he made the sign of the cross over you and said, "I absolve you of your sins, in the name of the Father, and of the Son, and of the Holy Spirit," which even in its total wrongheadedness, was so completely sweet.

The rape joke is that you were crazy for the next five years, and had to move cities, and had to move states, and whole days went down into the sinkhole of thinking about why it happened. Like you went to look at your backyard and suddenly it wasn't there, and you were looking down into the center of the earth, which played the same red event perpetually.

The rape joke is that after a while you weren't crazy anymore, but close call, Miss Geography.

The rape joke is that for the next five years all you did was write, and never about yourself, about anything else, about apples on the tree, about islands, dead poets and the worms that aerated them, and there was no warm body in what you wrote, it was elsewhere.

The rape joke is that this is finally artless. The rape joke is that you do not write artlessly.

The rape joke is if you write a poem called Rape Joke, you're asking for it to become the only thing people remember about you.

The rape joke is that you asked why he did it. The rape joke is he said he didn't know, like what else would a rape joke say? The rape joke said YOU were the one who was drunk, and the rape joke said you remembered it wrong, which made you laugh out loud for one long split-open second. The wine coolers weren't Bartles & Jaymes, but it would be funnier for the rape joke if they were. It was some pussy flavor, like Passionate Mango or Destroyed Strawberry, which you drank down without question and trustingly in the heart of Cincinnati, Ohio.

Can rape jokes be funny at all, is the question.

Can any part of the rape joke be funny. The part where it ends—haha, just kidding! Though you did dream of killing the rape joke for years, spilling all of its blood out, and telling it that way.

The rape joke cries out for the right to be told.

The rape joke is that this is just how it happened.

The rape joke is that the next day he gave you *Pet Sounds*. No really. *Pet Sounds*. He said he was sorry and then he gave you *Pet Sounds*. Come on, that's a little bit funny.

Admit it.

from *The Awl*

Oldtime Ending

◇   ◇   ◇

*for Ed Roberson, Ted
Pearson & Fred Moten*

Reluctant light light's
evasion, faces lit. Soulin'
  one of them called it,
                       they
sat around the fire . . . Re-
ticulate eyelight, life
outliving childhood . . .
  Bottomless whimsy,
                    bot-
  tomline wisp . . . All atop
time running out, what
  the attendant buzz was,
                    gleam
  seen somewhere else,
  anyone else's eye . . . All
  to say they lay thrown out
of the car, sprawled at cliff's
                    edge.
  Their heads hit the dirt, they
saw stars . . . It seemed they
saw love's low claw, rims
  riding asphalt, road their
                    dis-
  tended redoubt . . . Saw
themselves thrown from

the car, remembering
                    when,
   skin's old regard more
   skin . . . The end of it
met the end of the world,
skid no out of which but
                         out,
   dead or passed out, un-
seen outside face they fell
                         in-
   side

                    •

   Their heads' hit of dirt
      launched feathers. The
boy-god with birdlegs
                    lashed
   out . . . A made-up
   tribe's tale of the tribe it
   was they were caught
in, careened against all
                    hope
   of coming thru but came
      thru. Moot consequence . . .
Moody surmise . . . "If any-
   one should ask what
                    this
   was," the what-sayer sang,
      "say it was one for the
road the road rejected, some-
   thing for Ed that Ed
                    might
   have said, something for
   Ted that Ted might've
said, something for Fred
                    that
   Fred might've said, any-
thing should anyone ask . . ."

So went the old-time ending,
                                                    un-

ending. *Something for*
_____ *that* _____ *might've*
said echoed *something*
for _____ *that* _____
                                    might
have said echoed *some-*
thing for _____ *that* _____
might've said, echoed
                                    with-
out end or
amen

                    _____

        Stories told wanting to
be where they pointed . . .
        Flames they sat encircling
telling tales . . . The telling
                                        come
to no end, they sat listen-
        ing, flame-obsessed, ears
blown on by the wind . . .
        What was it the singing
                                    said,
        they kept wondering.
Something about a crash,
        they thought . . . That the
what-sayer sang smoked
                                        out
        certainty, they were un-
        sure. Something about
rescue, they thought . . .
                                    No
sooner thought than it
        was time to get going.
Trip City loomed outside
                                    the

woods' theoretic rest,
bait they were bent on
                              reach-
ing that much
more

                    •

"A madman at the wheel,"
   they heard him whisper,
the boy-god's low-key
   invective to no avail.
                         Rocked
   from side to side, put
upon by chaabi, a madman
   at the wheel beyond a
                         doubt . . .
   Rocked from side to
side, a boat it might've
   been, the birdlegged boy
its masthead had it been, a
                         slur
   pulled at the side of his
mouth. This the ythmic
   trek to Trip City: car
no metaphor, inveterate skid
                         no
   allegory, the ditch they
ended up in literal, every-
   thing resolute, real . . . So
they thought or so they
                         said
   they thought. Thought
disputed it. Mr. P's law
   was that thought would
                         have
   none of it. So much of
what they said they thought
   thought refuted, Mr. P's

                              ac-
      complice, they complained . . .
      No sooner that than the
      skid they thought endless
         ended. No sooner that
                              as
      though complaint made it
      so . . . An increased im-
      munity came over them, what-
         said cover, thought's
                              qualm
      and rebuff, cover's what-
      said complaint . . . Cover's
         whatsaid compliance it was,
                              what-
         ever worked worked out ad
      hoc . . . The tale's torn cloth
      what all there was of it,
      the tale the tale's rending,
                              not
      enough. They awoke some
         other morning on some
      other side of morning, happy
                              to
         awake but happy-sad to be
      awake, unsure they were awake,
         surprised . . . They were get-
      ting to be chagrined again. No
                              one
         could say what they made
      of it, road gone from as it
      was, awoke from what . . .
      Sprawled in what was known
                              as
      aftermath, light's disguised
         arrival, light's abject ad-
      dress . . . Light looking into
                              which
      they could only squint, go

off the road where the
highway bent . . . That was
                                    the
way the story
went

from *Poet Lore*

An Etiquette for Eyes

◇   ◇   ◇

I don't know
if I wore glasses
when I met you

but I know
the last time
I saw you you

drank a drink
I bought you
with another

woman who
was far uglier
than I have

ever been. I have brown eyes, did I ever tell you?
Your eyes are too too blue, tell-all awful, and too
too pretty; you make all the girls swoon, and then
lament how harpies pound on your door, plucking
the very shingles off your roof, conducting through
their unanimous will a plot to kill your hive's queen,
fix a hose from the car's tailpipe to pump barnyard
dread straight into your ken, therefore you demand
I ought never wish to lie in your bed. I have black eyes,

did I tell you? But your eyes are damp blue, fingers in
winter blue, worrying about a prom date blue, never

washed a dish blue. Have I mentioned my eyes are
dead brown, dirt brown, stone brown, done with you
brown, screaming out in the streets I'm so drunk brown,
I'm just ignoring the noise rising up from streets asleep
brown? As in, as brown as dead leaves because my love's
eyes were dead brown and when he shouted down at
that drunk on the street that New Year's Eve from

my third floor window that drunk man called him
Whiskey Whore Boy. And his eyes were not wish-
wash blue, his eyes were mostly moss and trees,
not mojitos in a barroom, no, his eyes all gin-lit in
a hotel room on our last night were ice-cold, even
in his farewell he was bold, his eyes anyone might
have called plain, but they could at least cry. I am
sick to death of your blue eyes, fabric eyes, flower
eyes. I have brown eyes, plain and saying eyes behind

thick frames, glassy eyes handing themselves over
to you in buckets eyes, dig your hands into my black
soil eyes, my ugly eyes reaching into your eyes for
my twin eyes, look back at me eyes while your eyes
crawl the walls, cloud-blue, wandering off as milky
bosomed maids will look away from the eyes that
seek the crevices deep between their heavy breasts
that sway beneath the cows they bend to milk eyes.
Won't you have another drink from my silty yonder

eyes? I may look
plain but I've got
roses in my blood,

can bloom right
out the soil of these
here brackish eyes,

wander a limb across
the chest of your
country, unlock

the footlocker of your
desire with the tip
of my vine eyes.

from *Willow Springs*

Masticated Light

◊   ◊   ◊

In a waiting room at the Kresge Eye Center
my fingers trace the outline of folded money
and I know the two hundred fifty dollars there
is made up of two hundred forty-five I can't afford to spend
but will spend on a calm voice that can explain
how I can be repaired. Instead, the words *legally blind*
and *nothing can be done* mean I'll spend
the rest of the week closing an eye to the world,
watching how easily this becomes that.
The lampposts lining the walk home
are the thinnest spears I've ever seen, a row of trash cans
becomes discarded war drums, and teeth
in the mouth of an oncoming truck
want to tear through me. Some of me
always wants to be swallowed.

• •

The last thing my doctor said before I lost
my insurance was to see a vision specialist
about the way light struggles and bends
through my deformed cornea.
Before the exam I never closed my right eye
and watched the world become a melting watercolor
with the left. Before a doctor shot light
into the twitching thing, before I realized
how little light I could handle, I never
thought much of the boy who clawed up at me
from beneath my punches, how a fingernail scraped

the eye, or how it closed shut
like a door to a room I could never leave.

• •

I could see the reflective mesh of his shoes,
the liquor bottle tossed in an arc
even before it shattered at my feet, and I am embarrassed
at how sharp my eyes were, how deft my body,
my limbs closing the distance—how easily
I owned his face, its fear, and fought back tears—
all of it mine. I don't want to remember the eyes
that glanced over shoulder just before
I dragged him like a gazelle into the grass
that was a stretch of gravel and glass
outside a liquor store. How easily this becomes that.

• •

On a suspension bridge I close my bad eye
and it's like aiming through a gunsight;
even the good eye is only as good as whatever glass
an optometrist can shape. I watch sundown
become a mouth. Broad and black-throated,
it devours the skyline and every reflection.
Horns sprout from the head of my silhouette
rippling *dark, dark, dark* against the haze of water
and I try to squint that monster
into the shape of a man.

from *Ploughshares*

Parasol

◊ ◊ ◊

You could still become a queen.
When, a slip of a girl,

you directed trees
to lower their limbs,

neither fire ants nor sap
could stop your climb,

nor rain that lightly fell,
misting leaves.

Inside a story's spell,
you find your way back,

where a stone on a path waits
for you to stumble.

Like the kaleidoscope's contents,
time is jumbled, opening at will.

Now: a too-bright sun and you,
teetering on a wall,

parasol clutched tight as you tumble.
This parasol is, for a moment,

everything you've lost
and all that can console.

from *The Southern Review*

vivisection
(you're going to break
my heart)

◊   ◊   ◊

the frog ready for inspection, skin flaps
opened and pinned back, organs

arrayed for the taking—this is how
I approach you. and you. here, my spleen

for the squeezing. my intestine
to be strung out, perhaps wrapped

around the neck like a lariat. not
for the squeamish, my heart thudding

to be plucked out with a delicate thumb
and forefinger, dinner for the willing,

and beautiful, and broken. I am not smart
about love, is what I'm saying. not even

smart about whose face I will take
in my hands and press against my face

until we are a single organism. the mouth
is not an organ but I give it to you

anyway, I give it all away is what
I'm saying. I'm easy to adore. my torso

a life raft strung with Christmas lights
and full of all your favorite things, beer

and expensive cheese and songs
about leaving. I'm so beautiful

splayed out on this tray full of tar
and entrails. I'm so useful

I could be a meal for an army
of traumatized surgeons, I'm full-time

at this job of bleeding, my esophagus
a stripper pole or cocaine straw.

when I say *eat me* I mean
suck the bones clean, leave nothing

for the waiting, nothing for the vultures
or the travelers to come.

from *The Carolina Quarterly*

Sylt I

◊　◊　◊

Lie still, he says.

Like a dog on the beach
he starts digging
until the hole fills up with water.
He has already dug out two thighs of sand
when she finally asks, what's there,
convinced there's nothing.

There's nowhere he can kiss her where she hasn't already been kissed by the sun.

Every evening she goes to the ocean with her three sisters and their old father.
They strip in a row,
                    their bodies identical as in a paper garland.
Bodies that make you think of women constantly chopping vegetables
            —it is like living by the train station,
                                    their father swears—
and always putting the last slice into their mouths.

For her, there is not even a knife left in the whole house.
The sound of a cuckoo limps across the dunes.
She takes a beam of sunlight sharpened side by side with stones
and cuts with it
and you can tell her vegetables from the others'
by how they burn.

By now they already stand wrapped in cocoons of white towels,
her teeth, crossed out by a blue line of lips, chatter,
scratching the grains of salt. Her bitten tongue

bleeds out into the mouth a red oyster,
which she gulps, breathless.

Their father turns away to dry his cock,
but the girls rub their breasts and crotches openly,
their hands skilled at wiping tables,
their heads as big as the shadow of the early moon,
their nipples as big as the shadows of their heads,
and black so that their milk might look even whiter.

She, too, is rough and indifferent toward her full breasts,
as if she were brushing a cat off the chair
for her old father to sit down.
They drink beer in the northern light that illuminates nothing but itself.
Sailboats slip off their white sarafans
baring their scrawny necks and shoulders,
and line up holding on to the pier as if it were a dance bar.

It bothers her, what did he find there after all?
So she touches herself under the towel.
It is easy to find where he has been digging—
the dug-up spot is still soft.

The water is flat like fur licked down by a clean animal.
A bird, big even from afar,
believes the ocean is its egg.
So the bird sits on the ocean patiently
and feels it kick slightly now and then.

from *New Letters*

Selection from Tanka Diary

◇   ◇   ◇

I'm seeing lots of dead zebras lately
on floors of elegant homes pictured in
interior decorator magazines.

WE PROUDLY HARVEST RAINWATER—a sign
in a neighbor's yard. With a deep barrel
I could humbly and thankfully harvest rain.

Several homeowners organize a neighbor-
hood watch patrol after discovering used
rubbers discarded on their lawns.

Folded cardboard tent-shaped trap
hanging among dark leaves of the lemon tree
to capture the galling Mediterranean fly.

A profusion of oleanders—to beautify
the freeway and filter the air, though
leaf, stem, and blossom are all poison.

Dried-out snake on the road
I brought as a curiosity to the child—
who insisted we give it a proper funeral.

Urban tumbleweed, some people call it,
discarded plastic bag we see in every city
blown down the street with vagrant wind.

from *The Harvard Review*

EILEEN MYLES

Paint Me a Penis

◇   ◇   ◇

If the best thing the world discovered today is that at the inside
of the universe is a cat
I love your braids; I love your peaceful eating
I hate that the sum total effect of the schedule
was sadness. Do you read the schedule. Nope.
I'm jealous. If he used the same words
over and over in plays and movies and commencement
addresses is that wrong. Is it wrong. What if art is wrong.
Is there only one sun. Some planets have two.
When the rain was pouring I wanted to be in there
silent with you. In the dog's beady black gaze. In the room
with the sleeping dog. With you leaving the room.
I've stopped the rain, I've silenced you.
I think the story was that one woman had gotten
the painting from the other and they were dating
but she never paid for it and then she moved out.
The painting sat in the second floor window and the painter
saw it and demanded it back. No. So the painter wrote
Marie O'Shea give me back my painting and put
it in the window opposite. She's a mess. We call her
cunt face. Twat. When it blasted I asked you to put
your headphones on. The dog's wheezing. I think
smack in the middle of that time was a virus
and it gave itself to everyone freely. We learned that
everything was related to everything else. Just as everything
was getting more separate and no longer a simple bowl
of fruit everyone was dying of the same thing. Not everyone.
Later when they hit the buildings it was just like everyone
in the city felt it. Not the same. We felt the shake. The request

in the air was how are we all feeling it now. It wasn't the same.
It was like you kept breaking off another square of the
bar and tasting it. He came running back into the room.
He was *moaning*. And now he just stares. And the rain
starts up again. I've never been invited to one meeting.
Do they have them. I remember the time I was invited
and we went around the room saying how we came
to be here. I was invited and everyone
stared and they never let me know when they were
meeting again. She wore a yellow dress. Everyone's watching you. He stands
in the doorway watching you eat. It stopped.
I want the painting in the window. Yeah. And you can
really ask her questions when you get her alone. And you were reading all the
time. And you said it a lot, that you wanted one which
you don't remember. I guess I wanted one. Now some
people in that mysterious time there it goes again
decided to in a very dedicated way begin talking about it
because there wasn't enough of that. That part had waned. Otherwise
you could just take it off the walls, you could go to funerals
and get fucked. You could recite it so that all they saw
was you. Huge numbers of them banded together marching
slowly into the room. There's footage of us dancing. I wouldn't ask
the stars to be quiet but I'm closer to them now. She was so
smart. I'm serious. I bet she'd make a good one. Since I didn't grow
my own I'd like to see what she'd make me. If he demands that no
one tells theirs at the breakfast table I think he probably pulls
it out of his pajamas and slaps it on the table. Dreams to me are
always receding. It's the only perfection: it's vanishing, stoking my
appetite so I'm drawing it for you as it becomes less the experience
that just happens as I'm resurrecting it for you. I'm making it
for you. I'm asking her. Make it for me. I'd like that. I'm putting it
in real deep. Out there, where everyone is.

from *Green Mountains Review*

Release from Stella Maris

◊   ◊   ◊

"So you're saying there is no self?" I asked the doctor.
"Well . . ." he said. He took off his glasses and breathed
on the lens—for a moment an extraordinary radiance
hardened there, then he flicked it with his cuff.

He coughed, painfully, and swallowed hard.
At once you heard the other patients bickering
along their waxed corridors, and I counted myself
lucky to be alone with the master surgeon,
the one whose lab coat bulges with key rings.

Perhaps this *I* who still speaks
was just the experience
of watching snow fly in a dim window?

That might be a great happiness.

When the head rose, I rose also, when he pulled on
his gray calfskin gloves, I rubbed raw knuckles,
braced for the wind that blows from the mind itself.

from *FIELD*

Stanley Kunitz Ode

◊   ◊   ◊

Ninety-five years before he died,
Stanley found an abandoned kitten
in the woods of Worcester. Stanley's father
had drunk Drano in a public park, while
Stanley had still been turning, a nebula
slowly taking human form
inside his mother. And when he found
the lost cat, he took it home
and gave it a box in the attic, under
the stars where his father was wheeling, and he raised
his feline companion—I don't know girl
or boy—without his mother much noticing,
hard as she worked, silent as she kept.
And his pet grew, and when they got to the woods he would
take off the collar and leash and they would
frolic together, she-he/he-she would
teach Stanley, already sinuous,
to slink and hunt. And I don't know who it
was who suddenly saw that Stanley's
companion, growing stronger and bigger and
lither, was a bobcat, and none of us
was there the night Stanley released her-him
or there when it rose in him, the desire
to seek a feline of his own species.
And when he was 98, and Elise
had gone ahead, leaving her words and
images behind her, casting the skin of them,
I saw, in a city in Ohio, an elegant
shaving-brush-soft replica bobcat,

and brought it back to West 12th, along with the
usual chocolates, and flowers, and a demo of my
latest progress toward a model's sashay on the catwalk.
And after that, when I'd come over, in those
outfits I wore then, Diana-ing
for a man, Stanley would be holding the stuffed
animal, and petting it,
nape to rump, nape to rump,
stub of the bob tail—98,
99, 100, those huge old beautiful
hands, stroking the world, which hummed when Stanley stroked it.

from *The Harvard Review*

Wishing Well

◇   ◇   ◇

Outside the Met a man walks up sun
tweaking the brim sticker on his Starter cap
and he says pardon me *Old School* he
says you know is this a wishing well?
Yeah *Son* I say sideways over my shrug
at the limpid smooth as spandex behind me.
        Throw your bread on the water.
I tighten my chest wheezy as Rockaway beach
sand with a pull of faux smoke from my e-cig
to cozy the truculence I hotbox alone
and I am at the museum because it is not a bar.
Because he appears not to have changed
them in days I eye the heel-chewed hems
of his pants and think probably he will
ask me for fifty cents any minute now wait
for it. A smoke or something. Central Park exhibits
the frisking transparency of autumn. Tracing
paper sky, leaves like eraser crumbs gum
the pavement. As if deciphering celestial
script I squint and purse off toward the roof
line of the museum aloof as he fists two
pennies from his pockets mumbling and then
aloud my man he says hey my man I'm going
to make a wish for you too.
        I am laughing now so what you want
me to sign a waiver? He laughs along ain't
say all that he says but you do have to
hold my hand.   And close your eyes.

I make a sabbath of my face before
he asks are you ready. Yeah *dawg* I'm ready.
Sure? Sure let's do this his rough hand
in mine inflates like a blood pressure cuff and I
squeeze back as if we are about to step together
from the sill of all resentment and timeless
toward the dreamsource of un-needing the two
of us hurtle sharing the cosmic breast
of plenitude when I hear the coins blink against
the surface and I cough up daylight like I've just
been dragged ashore. See now
you'll never walk alone he jokes and is about
to hand me back to the day he found me in
like I was a rubber duck and he says you got to let
go but I feel bottomless and I know he means
well though I don't believe
          and I feel myself shaking
my head no when he means let go his hand.

from *Painted Bride Quarterly*

Story Problem

◇   ◇   ◇

Suppose: a Device for measuring subdural space.
Let your Device be audible in all nightmares.
Suppose: all nightmares stick to the nerves & veins.
All veins get injured. Let that be true.
It's a great honor to get injured in a nightmare.
The honor is: you can activate your Skeleton-Gear.
Let X equal the force of your Skeleton-Gear striking a Life Token.
Let M equal the length of one nightmare.
Now multiply your Devices.
The shearing pain in your head comes from linear force.
You must have filled your head with Life Tokens.
Or: you've kicked a headful of Tokens with linear force.
Try to locate your Life Token without touching it.
Try to release your Life Token without locating it.
Then press ESC to affix your nightmare to a plane.
Your Device will jangle when it's ready to start affixing.
Let your nightmare expand along the inside of your Skeleton-Gear.
It's true that some nightmares have flags.
Indicate your readiness by smashing a handful of turf.
Collect: the Feelings Token.
Collect: the Flag Token.
You can step right out at any time.

from *The Baffler*

See You Later.

◇　◇　◇

The virus, your gentleman caller, pays his vulgar respects. We'll work from a
　　composite sketch. Send out a dragnet.
The thing is, those creatures can hide. Oviparous inside your ear canal they
　　hatch in your cochlea spiral & spiral.

How did he get inside? *Jimmy, oh Jimmy, oh Jimmy Mack, why don't you* cut the
　　lock. Somebody's mocking me.
He's like yesterday's newspaper: Sure you'd pick him up in a bathroom. But
　　you already know his type.

Hit the lights. Now who's at the door? It could be anybody. Let's call him
　　Jimmy now for continuity's sake.
Jimmy's not going to give us his specimen without we got a warrant. You're
　　going to have to catch him in the act.

from *The Iowa Review*

ROGER REEVES

The Field Museum

◊   ◊   ◊

It is customary to hold the dead in your mouth
Next to the other dead and their failing trophies:
Quetzal, starthroat, nightjar, grebe, and artic loon:
This ash for my daughter's tongue, I give without
Sackcloth or sugar: the museum closing,
The whale falling from heaven due
Upon our heads at any time: our haloes already
Flat as plates and broken about our ankles:
How often can you send a child to meet a ghost
At the river before the child comes back speaking
As the river, speaking as the pedal-less red
Bicycles half-buried in its bank, speaking bolt oil
Spilling down the legs of a thrice-trussed bridge
Just after a train lurches toward a coast covered in smog:
The river must be thick with this type of body:
A daughter bearing bird names on her lips, cutting
Her ankles on cans that resemble her mother's tongue.

from *The Cincinnati Review*

DONALD REVELL

To Shakespeare

◊   ◊   ◊

He made a statue of the east wind
Reconciled never too late, in
Silhouette, never too late as these
First days of March turn backward,
Facing the full of winter in
Enduring love, full jollity
Of winter's face to reconcilement,
In silhouette.

          He did not forget
Who lost his life to remember it.
Step down. Do not be proud.
There is a double heart behind
The breast bone. Bare it. Beat it.
Begin to eat it in full view,
Who loves you every inch of the wind.
First days of March, lords of jollity.

from *The Literary Review*

You Cannot Go to the God You Love with Your Two Legs

◇   ◇   ◇

And because you're not an antelope or a dog
you think you can't drop your other two limbs down
and charge toward the Eternal Heart. But
those are your legs too, the ones that have hauled
your strangest body through a city of millions
in less than a day, at its own pace, in its own pain,
and because you cannot make the pace of the one whom you love
your own, and because you cannot make the pain of the one you love
your own pain, your separate aches must meet somewhere
poised in the heaven between your bodies
—skylines turned on their sides—reminders
of what once was, what every man and woman
must build upon, build from, the body, the miserable,
weeping body, the deep bony awkwardness of love
in the bed. If you've kissed bricks in secret
or fallen asleep where there was no bed or spent time
lighting a fire, then you know the beginning of love
and maybe you know the end of it too,
and maybe you know the far ends, the doors, where
loved ones enter to check on you. It's not someone else speaking
when you hear *I love you*. It's only the nighttime
pouring into the breast's day. Sunset, love. The thousand
exits. The thousand ways to know your elbow
from your ass. A simple dozen troubled hunters

laying all their guns down, that one day
they may be among the first to step
into your devastated rooms
and say *Enough now, enough.*

from *Gulf Coast*

Saga

◊   ◊   ◊

Everything that ever happened to me
is just hanging—crushed
and sparkling—in the air,
waiting to happen to you.
Everything that ever happened to me
happened to somebody else first.
I would give you an example
but they are all invisible.
Or off gallivanting around the globe.
Not here when I need them
now that I need them
if I ever did which I doubt.
Being particular has its problems.
In particular there is a rift through everything.
There is a rift running the length of Iceland
and so a rift runs through every family
and between families as a feud.
It's called a saga. Rifts and sagas
fill the air, and beautiful old women
sing of them, so the air is filled with
music and the smell of berries and apples
and shouting when a gun goes off
and crying in closed rooms.
Faces, who needs them?
Eating the blood of oranges
I in my alcove could use one.
Abbas and ammas!
come out of your huts, travel
halfway around the world,

inspect my secret bank account of joy!
My face is a jar of honey
you can look through,
you can see everything
is muted, so terribly muted,
who could ever speak of it,
sealed and held up for all?

from *Court Green*

Decoded

◇　◇　◇

You / I
　　take / nurture
　　　　my / your
　　　　　　bag / blood
　　　　　　　and / and
　　　　　　　　pour / fill
　　　　　　　　　its / your
　　　　　　　　contents / emptiness
　　　　　　　　　on / from
　　　　　　　　　　the / the
　　　　　　　　　sidewalk / sky

If / When
　I / I
wear / undress
　　my / your
　　hoodie / skin
　　　　it / it
　　　is not / is
　　　　　in / from
　　　　danger / safety
　　　　　it / it
　　　is not / is
　　　　　in / from
　　　solidarity / alienation
　　　　　it / it
　　　　　is / is not
　　showmanship / reality

The / A
Interviewer / God
asked / answered
if / when
I / I
studied / neglected
how / why
Buddy Holly / Little Richard
disarmed / provoked
all / one
black / white
audiences / emptiness

My / Your
primary / final
album / silence
in / on
middle / infinite
school / repeat
was / is
Warren G's / Kenny G's
Regulators / lawlessness

"If / When
I / you
had / lose
a / the
son / moon
he'd / it
look / blinds
like / unlike
Trayvon" / anything

Our / Your
children / ancestors
will / won't
be / be
responsible / forgiven
for / despite
the / any
debts / surplus
we / you
have not / have
paid / assumed
in / from
blood / myths

The / A
white / black
girl / boy
on / in
stage / reality
said / listened
she / he
prayed / knew
Trayvon / Trayvon
reached / left
for / despite
the / a
gun / prayer

from *Rattle*

STEVE SCAFIDI

Thank You Lord for the Dark Ablaze

◊   ◊   ◊

For the deer gut busted open splayed
on the gravel margin of the highway
to remind me and to horrify which are
the same when death comes to say
anything for dying is a song the body
is learning so thank you lord for this
enduring whir of days we ride the way
a chisel carves down deep as it glides
for being is a lathe and we are the turning
curving shape of what I come to praise
so thank you Lord for the edge of light
when the day is honed and all is bright
behind the eyes just before waking for
dream is a fire we are the lake of—
dream is the spire we are the church
of—and the days turn so fast meaning
rattles hard and nearly breaks off—so
thank you lord for what arrives today
crashing down without a warning like
a pick-up truck on the deer this morning
or the morning light lashing me while
the sun flickers churning through the trees
like a wheel splashing rays on the redbud
dappling this holy thing I stand beneath
and I stand beneath and that is all, for
green is the mind of the spring returning

and dying a song the body is learning
which I will not sing or step to although
every day—oh—that is exactly what I do.

from *ABZ Poetry Magazine*

To Philip Roth, for His Eightieth

◇ ◇ ◇

I'm Mussolini,
And the woman spread out on my enormous *Duce* desk looks teeny.
The desk becomes an altar, sacred.
The woman's naked.

I call the woman teeny only because I need the rhyme.
The shock of naked looks huge on top of a desktop and the slime.
Duce! Duce! Duce! is what girls get wet with.
This one's perhaps the wettest one's ever met with.

Mussolini often did this,
Boots on, on the desk he worked at.
I'm sitting in my desk chair staring at *IT* and Oh she likes that.
She likes me staring at her box office.

Isn't everything theater? That's what's real.
I've got the face of an anteater
That sticks out like a penis to eat a meal.
I'm a chinless, cheater, wife-beater attending the theater.

It has to be someone else's wife.
Of course!
I live alone with my life.
One divorce for me was enough divorce.

I think of the late Joe Fox and his notion
That he couldn't sleep without a woman in his bed.
He also loved the ocean
And published Philip Roth when filthy Philip first got read.

When pre-spring March snow soft-focuses the city,
And the trees express their branches like lungs showing off their bronchi,
And the lined-up carriage horses stomp their hooves and whiten patiently,
I stay chained to my desk, honky honking honky.

from *London Review of Books*

Free Beer

◇ ◇ ◇

I'm the one who can hold a mouthful of salt.
Bring him here, the fool dressed in prison stripes.
I can pray for him, even though his eyes are wild.
I can de-louse the rat.

When I was a kid I invited them all to a puppet show.
There were no puppets; I'd planned no show.
Free beer, I said, and they came.

I've seen a puppet theater.
It resides in the black cavern behind my eyes.
Thoughts are puppets, dangling from their tangled strings.
Bring him here, the one spinning on gloom's rotisserie.

I'll section an orange for the wretched bastard.
I'll ladle him up a mugful of tears.
Free beer, I'll say, though there is no beer.

from *The Missouri Review*

I Grade Online Humanities Tests

◇   ◇   ◇

at McDonald's where there are no black people
and there's a multiple choice question
or white people about Don Quixote
or Asian or Indian people I don't want to be around
people I want to be here where there is
free wireless I do not want to sit at the Christian
coffee shop nor the public
library No I want religion to blow itself up
My sister converted to Catholicism
I do not want to sit at Starbucks
I like McDonald's coffee because it is cheap
and watery I like how it tastes
I like this table where the old man
is telling his old friend
about the baby black swan that he would feed
corn to in Cairo, Georgia, when he was a kid
No, Mark Twain did not write *Don Quixote* I'm going to
be here a while in this fucked up shit
You can get an old Crown Vic police car
In Cairo for $500 so I read
a poem by James Franco in the literary magazine I brought with
My mechanic wants to fuck me
And the poem isn't as bad
as people say he is bad One of his friends dies
in the poem He uses the word "cunt" I don't know
what to make of it I read it as "Cnut,"

the medieval prince of Denmark who ascended and ascended
to become the king of England I bet some managers here could relate
to Cnut Send me a pic of your
cunt the mechanic says I miss you I say what do
you miss about me He says "your big tits"
Elliott Smith is mentioned in
the Franco poem and might or might not
be a "cowboy" Maybe Franco really
is bad after all The Crown Vic is
a vehicle the way the police always
say "vehicle" not "car" but the mechanic
always says "car" not "vehicle" because I teach
the police I know how they talk The mechanic
says Sandra, stop speeding and do you want
to see a picture of my wife No, Cervantes
did not write "Because I Could Not
Stop for Death" and I will be
sitting here all day in this fucked up shit god
dammit click click click I keep looking
at things like pictures of your husband
which makes me feel sick
and watery Now a young boy, maybe 8 or 10
in a booth across from me
is telling his mamma his daddy's new girlfriend is ugly
"She's ugly, mamma" and trying to comfort her
Do you want to meet in the Home Depot
parking lot? I don't think this is a good
If I find you with him I'll kill him
and I'll kill you and no one will
know where your body But your husband
isn't ugly he is beautiful leaning over to look at himself
in pond water or leaning over
masculinity itself leaning over the family
he has made for himself and the pond
is male because he owns the pond
and the guns are male because he owns the guns
and what's happening is male because he owns the factors
that go into the car is male because he owns the police
and Home Depot is male because he owns and owns
and owns and all he can do is own

everything that will rot
like privacy or speech or porn or black swans
or my big tits which he misses
Fucking swans! A man decides to sit
next to me and he is frantically hitting
his Egg McMuffin on the table and then walks
outside and smokes a cigarette and returns
to his seat and starts hitting
his wrapped Egg McMuffin again
and then he sees my computer and asks
to check his Facebook so I let him
and then he wants to be friends on Facebook
and leaves his phone number on my page
and I "like" it and then in the background
the little boy's like "She's ugly, mommy
She's so ugly mommy" and the mom
is like "Is she? Is she ugly?" And I think the mom
is ugly even though I don't want her to be
and the other kids at the booth
are drinking milk and they are chubby
and eating fries and saying
"Yeah she's ugly
Yeah mommy she's so ugly
You wouldn't want to meet her
because she's so ugly"

from *The Awl*

JANE SPRINGER

Forties War Widows, Stolen Grain

◊   ◊   ◊

For decades we'd witnessed dark murders
        descend through crop-facing windows—
    so left our eggs un-whisked in batter
            for chase from sheer anger, suds rising, hot
            faucet streams, we forgot our spatulas
            forging to skillets, despite smoke we
            flung coats on, knocked bills akimbo,
                squashed pajamas in galoshes—Christ
                Armageddon—we left our cats crouched
            feral at raw bacon's ledge as we winged
                doors free, fell to knees, field-edge, braced
12 gauges—shot the thieves.

Someone has to clean up the
                    shells, toss grease-soaked papertowels, lick
                the whisker, soap grass-stained knees,
                sweep fresh tracks, fish the envelope
                spilled down floor vent despite ash &
                throw open the sash, zero out the still-
                flaming gas, trash the molten utensil, hang
                suds-logged rugs, straighten curtains on
        the kitchen Idyll, from sheer obligation—
    remake morning, scrub the afternoon clean,
    search the crop-facing window—though the
crows were the only things we ever got back.

from *Birmingham Poetry Review*

During the Autopsy

◇   ◇   ◇

"She hid it well," they say, gathered around the body. Some standing
in the gallery think of their god, big as an ox, and are thankful

for once not to be the chosen one. Her stomach opened to reveal
the tree growing inside her, seeming to take root near the navel,

branching out between the ribs. Thick bark falling away under
the scalpel. A man worries a pair of bats from her throat. Wings

raw from rubbing against the wood, panicky. Flesh houses
milk-white bulbs, new life, pale like her throat, a nice one.

A throat to be stroked nightly by some woodsman. And the bats
are the most vibrant black the man has ever seen. Their wings

seem to be living separately from their bodies, trying to detach.
And so he pictures the woman in the same light, tree its own

creature, not hers, not *her*, as he takes a bone saw to a branch,
or, with the smaller ones, snaps them off with his hands.

One must, at times, learn to ignore the body. In a dream
the man was once patron saint of ships. Not only did he build

the most seaworthy ships of his small town, but he blessed
all the vessels in the shipyard. Walking from wood hull to wood

hull, he would press his hands against them, speak to them with his
palms. And they would speak back. The man would carry their

stories with him from sleep, so that, in the morning, his hands were
still full with them, seemed to anchor him to the mattress, hands

heavy with whale bones and kelp nests. With crates of rotting
fruit, the smell of too many men together, skin sloughing off

like flakes of *sel de mer*. And the man had forgotten all this, until
his hands were around the trunk, growing like his own thigh,

and he could see each layer of the cut-into wood, which looked
not unlike each layer of the thick skin of the belly, the woman

not a woman, but a tree now. The tree, with his hands around it,
sang into him a high-pitched song, song of a siren, a woman's

voice asking to be returned to the sea. Any sea. And as he
washed his hands after, thorough as always, as he walked

home in the rain to his wife. As he drank the glass of water
she had poured him from a clay pitcher, he could feel that voice

in his throat, and that night he woke—suddenly, salt water
covering his entire body—to that other woman's song.

from *The Southern Review*

Passing Through
Indian Territory

◊   ◊   ◊

On horseback, I tell them to imagine me on horseback
going back to Boston, an oversized wool overcoat on top
of layers of things that make themselves warm against me,
old tops of boxes of pictures of horses pressed flat
to mesh and weave like cloth, I tell them it might take me
a few months to get home because I like to stop when I travel,
pull over so I can rest, and what about falling asleep
on the horse, what about what I did not imagine, smokestack
man slumped down snoring in the saddle, sliding over
to the edge of the grace of horses, their mercy, forgiveness
even for people who forget how the lines between territories
are made of the flesh of ghosts who had no words for where
land ends or where land begins or why there is a horse
waiting for me to answer for the uncle who killed her.

from *The New Yorker*

Sowing

◊   ◊   ◊

*. . . she glided from the sky and ordered him / to plow the ground
and then to plant within / the earth, the serpent's teeth: these were
to be / the seeds of men to come . . .*
—Ovid, *The Metamorphoses*

*. . . I can't make up / a name like Turnipseed! Or that // I knew
a man who went by such / a goodly name. . . .*
—Maurice Manning

I knew a man by such a name, though didn't know
        until you told me so, that a turnip seed is tiny, *it's
a little bit of hardly anything.* I should have known.
        Miniscule—a man, a goodly man, his seed—
what's that beside a war, misrule, history looming
        like a tower that throws its shadow
as it blocks the sun—the way (an old
        story) sin is cast on those most sinned
against; their coffins covered with a flag:
        stripes like the backs of slaves back when,
and stars—perhaps the last thing that you see
        when the landmine takes you—life and
limb, as the saying goes. My God. I knew a man,
        hardly more than a boy, though the word's
forbidden when the young man's black,
        as if you meant him disrespect. But he wasn't yet
out of his teens, a sweet kid name of Turnipseed,
        Carl as I recall, and I've always wondered how
the war turned out for him. Afraid, in fact, to know.

Showed up in class one day in uniform, but not
        to stay—to say goodbye—resigned, a fatalist.
Why struggle in a net that tightens
        when you fight its hold? Just say *so long*, and go.
All I could find to say was, please, take care
        of yourself. I mean, what good are words. *A little
bit of hardly anything.* And seeds?

What good, as they said in 'Nam, when you
        bought the farm—the field plowed with dragonseed,
from which those fratricidal armies sprang
        and fell upon each other's throats, and fell like dominoes
to join the ranks of headstones, *row on row on row* . . .
        And Turnipseed? That seed was meant to grow.

from *The Hampden-Sydney Poetry Review*

DAVID WOJAHN

My Father's Soul Departing

◊　◊　◊

> *Little soul, charismatic vagabond,*
> *Honored guest, comrade of the body.*
> *Now you shall depart into those regions*
> *Fogbound, anesthetized, and barren.*
> *Here your laughter served you well.*
> *There, everlasting, your mouth's stitched shut.*
> > —Hadrian, "Animula"

Assume, dear vagabond, you are permitted
　　One last survey. Your 21 grams of sentience,
　　　　Little soul—the weight exactly

Of a ruby-throated hummer—shall hover
　　The foliated stamens of your
　　　　Earthly measure. How you dart & pivot,

Honored guest, your thirst unquenchable.
　　Here is Milbank, South Dakota,
　　　　The saffron dustbowl where your father,

Dear comrade, raises his belt to crisscross your back:
　　The five & twenty lesions. Here the state hospital,
　　　　Your mother ballooning with insulin

To induce the coma meant to cure the demons
　　Marauding the precincts of her abject brain.
　　　　Now you shall depart: a milk run in Duluth,

A quart bottle bursting on a frozen stoop, then
    A troop ship bound for Tunis, & into those regions
        Of desert where you wander your forty days.

You rifle the pockets of a dead Wehrmacht corporal:
    Luger & a snakebite kit. & now you lean
        From a baggage car door, hefting a postal sack

As the train slows for a station—Breckinridge
    Or Sleepy Eye—slows but will not stop
        For twenty-seven years. The railroad men's

Hotels along the tracks, pulls of bourbon
    From a dented flask. The white Dakota plains—
        Fogbound, anesthetized & barren.

Montage of seven Chevy Biscaynes, the songbook
    Of Ernest Tubb. A shingled ranch, deriving from
        The GI Bill. GARDEN SIX TWO FOUR

SEVEN SEVEN, the receiver lifted from its cradle
    As you weep to a stranger who's purloined
        Your pension. Pulls of bourbon

From a highball glass, from a coffee cup, the thrall
    & ratchet of ECT, your dress rehearsal
        For oblivion. What I remember: your laughter

Did not serve you well. Honored guest, comrade
    Of the body, your farewell is complete.
        Blessèd the descent which beckons.

There, everlasting, your mouth's stitched shut.

from *AGNI*

Detainment

◊   ◊   ◊

In the undisclosed desert facility, they strapped me
to a steel table and told me to recite the poem that
would save the world.

(I had arrived there in a windowless, automated van
driven inside the hollow mountain—

through the forest they had chased me to exhaustion.)

They polished metal tools I'd never seen before.

To break me down, at first one of them kept
tapping on my nose and whispering lyrics,
access codes, rapid sequences of Greek letters
and English surnames.

One tried to interface with my brain, injecting a sort
of horned electrode into Wernicke's, then Broca's.
My larynx in spasm. My hands were hooves, then
nightingale beaks, the fluorescent tubes above me
were my white bones.

I chanted baby names during sensations of drowning,
overwhelming nausea. Back and forth from ice-cold
water, mock burials. They crowned me with electrified
laurels.

They touched me, laughing.

They touched me and I sang and for what?

from *Cream City Review*

Blessed Are

◊   ◊   ◊

You, faithful ravens, staying on and saying
through the songbirdless winter
the biblical syntax of your declarations.

It is with great fascination I watch you excise,
with inordinate patience, the upward eye
of the fallen deer below the house.

I confess the sight through my binoculars
puts me eye-to-eye with both you
and the eye you eat and squabble over,

gustatory, opening now and then your great wings
in contretemps corvidae vexations,
like a scrum of omnivorous umbrellas.

Further plunder will require your partners, the coyotes,
slinking even now your way and awaiting
the night your plumage exemplifies

and under which they will open the carcass
for your further delectation and caws
the dozen mornings I imagine it will take.

Then the snows will bury it, and many mice
will gnaw its bones until it emerges yet again
from the melts of spring, a blessing for the blowflies

and the seethe of their maggots, until the vault
the empty brain occupied is emptied itself,
and I retrieve the skull and hang it on my shack.

There it will be filled with the thoughts of yellow jackets,
there it will grin its grim, unmandibled
half-smile out over the distances swallows

troll for the yellow jackets themselves,
and one of you will perch yourself upon a bare rib then,
to recite, for the world, your ravenous beatitudes.

from *Southern Indiana Review*

Calendar Days

◇ ◇ ◇

One day you wake and they're there, flecks of mud
weed-eaters throw against the window, moths
in their dark migrations, salmon that taste like dust.
All month long, they fall from the laundry, dead
receipts for burritos, coffees, books. They've lotused
toilet water, drinks left out from the night before.
They rifle into floodlights, their exit wounds
so much skin, so much powdered glue. April's cruelty
is, isn't it, just a rumor floated by May and June
while everyone fans the rice pages of their Bibles
in sermons' hot wind. It's the dry air makes them rise.
In these parts now they say *sirocco*, entirely
out of place. They say *monsoon*, which is a way
of not saying fire, virga, *haboob*. I'd like to feel
the milt wind off Erie or Ontario, fresh strawberries
and airlift oysters to chew, but I've got to rise again
to pull the locust beans from the choking gutters,
which I explain as a prayer for rain. Tomorrow's
my birthday day in another month, a twelfth
of a reminder of something I can't remember,
though they say I was there, Polaroid, Panavision
images dreamed or dreamed for me, half-holy
half-haunted, like the streets of Jackson slowly going
Kodachrome, gelatin silver, dim,
my father's menthol still reporting in the tray.
You have to look away so the smoke's cursive's
written clear, my grandmother's card, her best
farmer's Palmer method, *Our pride & joy*,
flutter of money, even after all these years,

take the day off. But there are bills to pay,
even without stamps, days in advance
so they'll post on time, someone born or someone
dying so near midnight, one day's clocked,
the next not yet in. It takes a while to sort it out.
You may already be a winner. I check, of course,
the numbers each day, though I've often forgotten
to buy a ticket, as my father reads the obits to see
if he's still alive. It would be a great excuse,
he says, call in dead for work. In the joke, God says
give me a chance. You should know, he says,
the trade-in on your car in case you want to ditch
it in a quarry, set it on fire, though the heat's never
hot enough to melt it back to stone. The fireflies
rise from the evening grass, whispering in a language
I mistake for fire, into the boughs, a few
floating higher than hunger, toward the stars.
There, the bears move slow as days,
so slow sometimes I forget what day it is.
And sometimes, thank God, they go on forever.

from *The Missouri Review*

DEAN YOUNG

Emerald Spider
Between Rose Thorns

◊   ◊   ◊

Imagine, not even or really ever tasting
a peach until well over 50, not once
sympathizing with Blake naked in his garden
insisting on angels until getting off the table
and coming home with my new heart. How absurd
to still have a body in this rainbow-gored,
crickety world and how ridiculous to be given one
in the first place, to be an object
like an orchid is an object, or a stone,
so bruisable and plummeting, arms
waving from the evening-ignited lake,
head singing in the furnace feral and sweet,
tears that make the face grotesque,
tears that make it pure. How easy
it is now to get drunk on a single whiff
like a hummingbird or ant on the laughter
of one woman and who knew how much I'd miss
that inner light of snow now that I'm in Texas.

from *Poetry*

148

Mindful

◇   ◇   ◇

jammed my airspace w/ an audible.com podcast

& to-do list Deborah lent me this pen better
make use of turn off it filled up inside dear friends
[*swipe again*] invite me to Brooklyn [*swipe
again*] I briefly [*GO*] hate them am rush rush &
rushing headphones never let me airways
I run & the running [GPS: *average time*]
[*activity started*] [GPS: *per mile*] then a snow-
storm no school I cried & said *Mayor Bloomberg
should be scalded with hot cocoa* when someone said
yay for snow I'm cutting it too close, Erin, if
a blizzard makes me [*too slow swipe again*]
cry I used to [*activity started*] long for snow
that quiet filling everything up what is time for
anyway? Jeremy says *It's funny how* [*Too Slow*]
[*same turnstile*] *"work" in your poems is a metaphor
for* [*Go*] [*Go*] [*Go*] [*Go*] [*Go*] *"free time"* [*same
turnstile*] "free time" what's that? is it NY? *What
are you talking about?* asks Erin, *Seriously what
are you talking about?* [*1 X-fer*] [*total time*] [*average
time*] [*GO GO GO GO*] crammed in the tiny bed
Still I say *If you want me to stay, you need to lie still*
the toddler tries why? must he? [*X-fer*] [*X-fer*]
[*all service on the local track*] fall asleep fast I pray
to whom? [*1 X-fer ok*] is this what I was
waiting for: the one nap moment of silence?
if that's what I wanted should have made other
don't you think choices? *What do you mean*

by "dark"? asks Erin *What do you mean by "in-*
tolerable"? "unhinged"? airways [GO] I give one son
a quarter for two or fewer complaints a day
& none for more the pediatrician confirms
they each have two testicles then shoots
the smallest boy in the arm that was the easiest
part of my day [*X-fer OK*] [*OK*] [*OK*] [*GO*] stroller
is it the lack of human [*X-fer*] contact? oh
please have no time for *that* got to go to sleep
by 10 pm or am up all night something about
circadian rhythms then it's toddler-early-waking
Still night! we tell him *Not time* timing time *Not*
time to wake up! we tell him *Go back* he won't
we're up it's dark is it too early to make lunch
or dinner? *What are you saying?* texts Erin *Can't*
talk I text back but want to say [*X-fer*] to ask
why is this life so run-run-run I run only thing
I can—free wasted time—control? long
underground F the train crosstown bus that
screaming is *my* son with his 50 small feet
kicking *Too slow bus!* screaming Meredith says
The breath is the only thing in your life that
takes care of itself does it? [*too fast*] [*same*
turnstile] Rebecca wanted us to do something
radical at this reading I don't have time did
wash my hair lifestyle choice I know time
isn't "a *thing* you have" I meant to ask isn't there
some way, Erin, to get more not time but joy?
she's not home maybe running or at the grocery
or school [*X-fer*] can you anyone hear me? my
signal pen airway failed Deborah lent me
this one GPS *time left* or *time left*—two
meanings—I've forgotten to oh! left my urgh!
meat in the freezer or oven on so what? don't
make dinner—ha ha who will? the military?—
don't rush multi-stop stop checking the tiny
devices brain sucking the joy out here's the
[*too fast*] [*swipe again*] [*OK*] express

from *The Kenyon Review*

CONTRIBUTORS' NOTES AND COMMENTS

SHERMAN ALEXIE was born in 1966 and grew up in Wellpinit, Washington, on the Spokane Indian Reservation. His first collection of stories, *The Lone Ranger and Tonto Fistfight in Heaven* (1993), won a PEN/Hemingway Award. In collaboration with Chris Eyre, a Cheyenne/Arapaho Indian filmmaker, Alexie adapted a story from that book, "This Is What It Means to Say Phoenix, Arizona," into the screenplay for the movie *Smoke Signals*, which won the Audience Award and Filmmakers Trophy at the 1998 Sundance Film Festival. His most recent books are the poetry collection *Face* from Hanging Loose Press, and *War Dances*, stories and poems from Grove Press. *Blasphemy*, a collection of new and selected stories, appeared in 2012 from Grove Press. *The Absolutely True Diary of a Part-Time Indian*, a novel, appeared from Little, Brown Books for Children. He is lucky enough to be a full-time writer and lives with his family in Seattle.

Of "Sonnet, with Pride," Alexie writes: *"Pride of Baghdad*, by Brian K. Vaughan and Niko Henrichon, is a graphic novel that tells the true story of a pride of lions that escaped during the Iraq War and were subsequently killed by U.S. soldiers. Well, I suppose 'true story' is a loose definition of the book since we enter into the minds of the lions and various other animals. In any case, it's a tragic novel. I have reread it often. And think of it quite often, too, so when Seattle's Recovery Café, a drug and alcohol addiction treatment facility for homeless and low-income people, asked me to write them a poem, I immediately thought of those lost and hungry lions. I don't often write occasional poems, and don't know that I'd ever written a good occasional poem, but this one seems to have lasting power. We're all soul-hungry, right? Well, this poem does its best to make us consider and reconsider the universal nature of soul-hunger."

RAE ARMANTROUT was born in Vallejo, California, in 1947. She is a professor of poetry and poetics at the University of California, San

Diego. Wesleyan University Press has published all her recent books. They include *Just Saying* (2013), *Money Shot* (2011), *Versed* (2009), and *Next Life* (2007). A new book, *Itself* (in which "Control" appears), will be published by Wesleyan in 2015. She has received the Pulitzer Prize.

Armantrout writes: " 'Control' begins with the experience of learning (or trying to learn) to meditate. The first stanza reproduces the instructor's advice that we should 'set obtrusive thoughts aside.' The third, fifth, and eighth stanzas develop my responses to this experience while the second, fourth, sixth, and seventh stanzas present the obtrusive thoughts as fragments of the debris field of American media culture. For instance, I recently heard a politician say, 'It takes an American to do really big things.' He was talking about our space program, which, of course, is being systematically defunded."

JOHN ASHBERY was born in Rochester, New York, in 1927. He has published more than twenty collections of poetry, most recently *Quick Question* (Ecco, 2012), as well as numerous translations from the French, including works by Pierre Reverdy, Arthur Rimbaud, Raymond Roussel, and several volumes of poems by Pierre Martory. *Collected French Translations*, a two-volume set of his translations (poetry and prose), was published in 2014 (Fararr, Straus and Giroux). He exhibits his collages at the Tibor de Nagy Gallery (New York). He was the guest editor of *The Best American Poetry 1988*, the initial volume in the series.

ERIN BELIEU was born in Omaha, Nebraska, in 1967. She has four poetry collections, all from Copper Canyon Press: *Infanta* (1995), *One Above & One Below* (2000), *Black Box* (2006), *Slant Six* (2014). She is a professor in the creative writing program at Florida State University and is a member of the poetry faculty at Lesley University's low-residency MFA program in Cambridge, Massachusetts. She is also cofounder of VIDA: Women in Literary Arts and the artistic director for the Port Townsend Writers Conference.

On "With Birds," Belieu writes: "The very best thing about our home in Tallahassee is that it's presided over by a three-hundred-year-old live oak. She's a beauty, with a trunk fifteen feet around and limbs that stretch two houses in either direction. Of course, because of her size, she also serves as a superhighway for the many critters living in north Florida's canopy.

"I work on our deck most mornings, and in that time I've been reminded often and none too gently how unromantic nature is. The impulse for 'With Birds' came when I heard a meaty thump and looked up to find a good-sized slab of bloody snake carcass lying decapitated on the deck next to me. No doubt one of the hawks or barred owls that surround our house was clumsy with breakfast that morning. There is also the issue of one particularly loud and luckless cardinal—a 'blast-beruffled plume' sort of fellow—who often shrieks nonstop pick-up lines from atop our fence while I'm trying to work. So I think of 'With Birds' as an affectionate complaint. But, really, I like having all the wild things around me."

LINDA BIERDS was born in Wilmington, Delaware, in 1945. She is the author of nine books of poetry: *Roget's Illusion* (Putnam's, 2014); *Flight: New and Selected Poems* (Putnam's, 2008); *First Hand* (Putnam's, 2005); *The Seconds* (Putnam's, 2001); *The Profile Makers* (Henry Holt, 1997); *The Ghost Trio* (Henry Holt, 1994); *Heart and Perimeter* (Henry Holt, 1991); *The Stillness, the Dancing* (Henry Holt, 1988); and *Flights of the Harvest-Mare* (Ahsahta Press, 1985). She has won the PEN/West Poetry Prize, the Consuelo Ford Award from the Poetry Society of America, the *Virginia Quarterly Review*'s Emily Clark Balch Poetry Prize, and fellowships from the National Endowment for the Arts, the Ingram Merrill Foundation, the Guggenheim Memorial Foundation, and the John D. and Catherine T. MacArthur Foundation. She is a Byron W. and Alice L. Lockwood Professor in the Humanities at the University of Washington in Seattle.

Of "On Reflection," Bierds writes: "For some time I've been interested in the scientist Michael Faraday, and I've been particularly enchanted by a series of lectures that he delivered in 1860 at the Royal Institution of Great Britain. Although written for children, the lectures attracted people of all ages, drawn by Faraday's enthusiasm and warmth, and by his conviction that common objects within our lives are often the best illustrators of scientific truths.

"One day I was looking through an old edition of *World Book Encyclopedia* and came across an entry on the mirror. The contributor's style was so similar to Faraday's, so clear and unassuming, that I could easily imagine Faraday repeating his words—and the poem was born. The pantoum form, with its mirroring lines, seemed a natural choice."

TRACI BRIMHALL was born in Little Falls, Minnesota, in 1982. She is the author of *Our Lady of the Ruins* (W. W. Norton, 2012) and *Rookery* (Southern Illinois University Press, 2010). Her work has received fellowships from the Wisconsin Institute for Creative Writing, the King/Chávez/Parks Foundation, and the National Endowment for the Arts.

Of "To Survive the Revolution," Brimhall writes: "Even as a child I was interested in the question of survival. I loved books in which young people had to learn wilderness skills in hopes of lasting long enough to be rescued. To my adult mind, the question has become a moral one—would I harm someone who was attacking me to ensure my own survival? Could I kill that person? Would I harm or kill someone who wasn't trying to do me harm if it meant I would live? This is the idea I engaged with in 'To Survive the Revolution.' The poem takes place during the Brazilian coup d'etat in the 1960s. I've tried to imagine my way into a life and set of circumstances that would force me to make that choice—whether to hurt someone else or die."

LUCIE BROCK-BROIDO was born in Pittsburgh, Pennsylvania, in 1956. She attended Johns Hopkins University where she earned her BA and MA in 1979. In 1982, she received her MFA in poetry from the School of the Arts at Columbia University. She has published four volumes of poetry, all with Alfred A. Knopf: *A Hunger* (1988), *The Master Letters* (1995), and *Trouble in Mind* (2004); her most recent collection, *Stay, Illusion* (Knopf, 2013), was a finalist for both the National Book Award and the National Book Critics Circle Award. She is also the editor of *Letters to a Stranger*, the collected poems of Thomas James (Graywolf Press, 2008). In 2010, Carcanet brought out her selected poems, *Soul Keeping Company*, in the United Kingdom. She has won a Guggenheim Fellowship, two National Endowment for the Arts Awards, the Witter-Bynner Prize from the American Academy of Arts and Letters, and the Massachusetts Book Award. She is director of poetry in the School of the Arts at Columbia and lives in New York City and Cambridge, Massachusetts.

Brock-Broido writes: "'Bird, Singing' is an elegy for the poet Jason Shinder. In real life, he was often known as 'Jay.' Many of his intimates called him Jay Bird. Over the years, I began to call him, simply: Bird. He was in flight all the time.

"One of the many gifts he left me: inside a tiny red & yellow box, there is an even smaller wicker cage, an architecture of elegance. Inside the cage, on a little wicker bar, there is a miniature song bird with a feathered tail. There's a key to wind up the creature, which—when wound—begins to sing until, in a few moments, his time runs out. Its song is so beautiful that, to this day, I can barely stand to listen to it. But I do.

"I've kept the box it came in, too. On the front, in gold letters, it says: *Songing Bird.* I have a hunch it was first written in Japanese, translated into French, through Yiddish, to Polish, through Russian, and, finally, into American.

"The gold bees in the poem came by way of Mandelstam. The term 'onion snow' refers to the last snowfall at the end of winter. You can know it was the last, of course, only in hindsight—once it is really spring. In the poem, somehow Bird & I wound up in April, and in Prague (where I have never been); I don't know how."

JERICHO BROWN was born in Shreveport, Louisiana, in 1976. He once worked as a speechwriter for the mayor of New Orleans (Marc Morial from 1998 to 2002 and Ray Nagin in 2002). Brown is an assistant professor at Emory University. His poems have appeared in journals and anthologies including *The American Poetry Review, jubilat, Oxford American, The New Republic, The New Yorker, Ploughshares,* and *100 Best African American Poems.* His first book, *Please* (New Issues Poetry & Prose, 2008), won the American Book Award, and Copper Canyon Press published his second book, *The New Testament,* in September 2014.

Brown writes: "I am ever fascinated by all the people who like 'Host' but have never met a man via jack'd, grindr, or adam4adam.com. I'm hoping this poem's appearance here lends power to my conviction that there is very little universal about poetry other than the marvelous music it makes in the mind and the mouth. And I trust this poem speaks for itself in its attempts to investigate desire, sexuality, and masculinity."

KURT BROWN (1944–2013) was the founding director of the Aspen Writers' Conference and founding director of Writers' Conferences & Centers. He served on the board of Poets House in New York for six years. He was the editor of *Drive, They Said: Poems about Americans and Their Cars* (1994), *Verse & Universe: Poems about Science and Mathematics* (1998), and coeditor with his wife, poet Laure-Anne Bosselaar, of *Night Out: Poems about Hotels, Motels, Restaurants and Bars* (1997). In addition, he was the editor of *The Measured Word: On Poetry and Science* (2001), and a coeditor of the tribute anthology for the late William Matthews, *Blues for Bill* (2005). He was also coeditor, with Harold Schechter, of *Conversation Pieces: Poems that Talk to Other Poems* (2007) and *Killer Verse: Poems of Murder & Mayhem* (2011). His first two full-length collections, *Return of the Prodigals* and *More Things in Heaven and Earth,* were published by Four Way Books. *Fables from the Ark* (WordTech) won the 2003 Custom Words Prize. His most recent collections, *Time-Bound* (2012) and *I've Come This Far to Say Hello: Poems Selected and New* (2014), were published by Tiger Bark Press. His memoir, *Lost Sheep: Aspen's Counterculture in the 1970s: A Memoir*, came out from Conundrum Press; and *Eating Our Words: Poets Share Their Favorite Recipes* is due out from Tupelo Press in 2014. With Laure-Anne Bosselaar he translated the Flemish poet Herman de Coninck's *The Plural of Happiness* (2006). He taught at Sarah Lawrence College, Georgia Tech, and Westminster College in Salt Lake City, Utah. He died in Santa Barbara, California, in June, 2013.

CAConrad was born on January 1, 1966. He is the author of six books, including *ECODEVIANCE: (Soma)tics for the Future Wilderness* (Wave Books, 2014), *A Beautiful Marsupial Afternoon* (Wave, 2012), and *The Book of Frank* (Wave, 2010). A 2014 Lannan Fellow, a 2013 MacDowell Fellow, a 2012 UCROSS Fellow, and a 2011 Pew Fellow, he conducts workshops on (Soma)tic poetry and Ecopoetics.

Of "wondering about our demise while driving to Disneyland with abandon," Conrad writes: "This poem is from a series I call *TRANS-LUCENT SALAMANDER*, forthcoming in *ECODEVIANCE: (Soma) tics for the Future Wilderness* (Wave Books, 2014). It was written at UCROSS Ranch in Wyoming, a magnificent artist residency where I constructed eighteen of my own constellations at night, later combing my constellation notes to locate the language for eighteen poems. I used crystals given to me by poets Elizabeth Willis and Bhanu Kapil when taking the initial notes, and for the editing process I would begin by eating fruit infused with music from Missy Mazzoli's now famous *Cathedral City* CD. I would infuse the fruit by placing my laptop on the floor with the fruit, then play a track of Mazzoli's music as loud as I could, covering fruit and laptop with a basket, then pillows, blankets, towels, and a large comforter. Then I would quickly eat the fruit and begin editing my constellation notes for the poems. We are all collaborators with one another in many ways, deliberate or not, and my poems are always a thank-you to everyone around me."

ANNE CARSON was born in Canada and teaches ancient Greek for a living. Her recent publications include *Red Doc* (Alfred A. Knopf) and *Nay Rather* (Sylph Editions).

Carson writes: "'A Fragment of Ibykos Translated 6 Ways' was an exercise in translation undertaken just to see where it would go. It was certainly the hardest thing I did all year."

JOSEPH CERAVOLO (1934–1988) was born in Astoria, Queens, and lived in New Jersey. He studied with Kenneth Koch at The New School. He was the author of six books of poetry and won the first Frank O'Hara Award. He earned his living as a civil engineer. The *Collected Poems* of Joseph Ceravolo, edited by Rosemary Ceravolo and Parker Smathers, was published in 2013 by Wesleyan University Press. "This haunting tome is a masterpiece, a complex concerto of poems moving on a visionary trajectory" (Anne Waldman).

HENRI COLE was born in Fukuoka, Japan, in 1956. He has published eight collections of poetry and received the Jackson Prize, the Kingsley Tufts Award, the Rome Prize, the Berlin Prize, and the Lenore Marshall Award. A new collection, *Nothing to Declare*, is forthcoming from Farrar, Straus and Giroux. He lives in Boston.

Of "City Horse," Cole writes: "I was trying to write a poem (about a dead horse) that was many things: vocal, autobiographical (but mythic-seeming), dramatic (within the framework of a single sentence), and with a headlong galloping full of romantic ambition, sadness, and white heat. I don't think I succeeded, but the striving was enough."

MICHAEL EARL CRAIG was born in Dayton, Ohio, in 1970. He earned degrees from the University of Montana and the University of Massachusetts. He is the author of *Talkativeness* (Wave Books, 2014), *Thin Kimono* (Wave, 2010), *Yes, Master* (Fence Books, 2006), *Can You Relax in My House* (Fence, 2002), and the chapbook *Jombang Jet* (Factory Hollow Press, 2011). He is a certified journeyman farrier and shoes horses for a living near Livingston, Montana.

Of "The Helmet," Craig writes: "As I understand it the female emu lays her eggs and leaves. The male then sits on them for two months, not eating this whole time, just sitting and losing weight. He keeps getting up to fuss over the eggs, rotating a bit before sitting back down in order to distribute the warmth more evenly, and if you try messing with the eggs this male emu might try to kill you. I'm telling you this because some poems are like eggs I have to sit on. Sometimes I sit on them too long maybe—revision after revision, nit-picking, obsessing. But this poem came quickly and I bet it had something to do with whatever I'd been writing right before it. This sometimes happens to me—a poem is a reaction to its immediate predecessor. A friend suggested I describe the helmet: what kind of helmet is this? But I think that's for the reader to decide. The word helmet is a powerful one. The whole concept, really. A shell to protect the head."

PHILIP DACEY is the author of twelve books of poetry, most recently *Gimme Five*, which won the 2012 Blue Light Press Book Award; *Mosquito Operas: New and Selected Short Poems* (Rain Mountain Press, 2010); and *Vertebrae Rosaries: 50 Sonnets* (Red Dragonfly Press, 2009). Born in 1939 in St. Louis, Dacey has written collections about Gerard Manley Hopkins, Thomas Eakins, and New York City. He has received a Discovery Award from the New York YM-YWHA's Poetry Center and various fellowships (a Fulbright to Yugoslavia, a Woodrow Wilson to Stanford, and two in creative writing from the National Endowment for the Arts). With David Jauss, he coedited *Strong Measures: Contemporary American Poetry in Traditional Forms* (Harper & Row, 1986). After an eight-year postretirement adventure in New York City, he returned in 2012 to Minnesota—where he taught for thirty-five years at Southwest Minnesota State University—to live in the Lake District of Minneapolis with his partner, Alixa Doom.

Dacey writes: "When I moved in 2004 from Minnesota to Manhattan's Upper West Side, I did not know the Juilliard School was in my neighborhood. I soon became a Juilliard junkie, attending recitals and concerts almost daily, sometimes more than once a day. Juilliard is one elite school where admission depends solely on the student's dedication and ability and not on parental status or influence; a president's son would not get in if he botched the audition piece. In summers, when Juilliard closed, I went into Juilliard-withdrawal. 'Juilliard Cento Sonnet' is meant to provide an inside look at music performance, at all the work and fine-tuning that goes on behind what may look effortless. I find that the technical, professional talk of musicians can be richly resonant, arguably itself a kind of poetry."

OLENA KALYTIAK DAVIS was born in 1963, in Detroit. As a child she was enlisted to recite poems, by heart and in Ukrainian, to small patriotic crowds, and she has had divided feelings about poetry and its practice since. Her latest collection, *The Poem She Didn't Write and Other Poems*, is out in 2014 from Copper Canyon Press. Her work has appeared in five earlier volumes of *The Best American Poetry* (1995, 2000, 2001, 2004, 2011), sometimes under D for Davis and sometimes under K for

Kalytiak. She lives in Anchorage, Alaska, practices some law, and raises her kids.

Of "It Is to Have or Nothing," Kalytiak Davis writes: "I don't really like this poem, which brings up all sorts of problematic ideas and emotions. It has some really good stuff in it, but doesn't really heighten and cohere. Giving myself some benefit of that doubt, much like the relationship / breakup it delineates. I guess the most interesting thing about the poem (other than any possible naming of / updated proclaiming to the *vital, arrogant, fatal, dominant X*) is all the other poems that really happen/ed in and around it: that they are actually part of the dirt! The title is a Wallace Stevens line—I had forgotten from which poem, but am glad it's 'Poetry Is a Destructive Force,' which I found in my 'chats' from that time; the first French words are from Rilke's ninth—which was reread out loud with a friend also during that time (the notion of speech over procreation?); the Coleridge, well, really, just for its title-in-lapness, which, yes (!), really happened; and, finally, repeatedly: 'Purple Bathing Suit,' which really was Sent. That really good poem, taken out of the context of *Meadowlands*, is often (automatically, autobiographically) mis-gendered: the man confusingly wearing, at least in my ugly mind, a disgusting little purple Speedo. As I now know: it was in fact a maillot, and it was hers/mine, and I did not look as good in it as I had thought."

Born in Ghana in 1962 and raised in Jamaica, KWAME DAWES is a poet, novelist, playwright, anthologist, musician, and critic. He is the author of more than thirty-five books, including eighteen books of poetry, and numerous anthologies. He is Glenna Luschei Editor of *Prairie Schooner* and Chancellor's Professor of English at the University of Nebraska-Lincoln. He is a faculty member of the Pacific MFA program in Oregon and a faculty member of Cave Canem. *Duppy Conqueror: New and Selected Poems* appeared with Copper Canyon Press in 2013.

Of "News from Harlem," Dawes writes: "Sometimes reading a play by August Wilson can be a transporting experience. You feel you have entered a different world, a different era, and place so intensely captured that you feel as if you are there. And so here I am reading *King Hedley II*, and I see the name Marcus Garvey, and I think, of course, there is Garvey, and then I imagine that in the midst of the day-to-day details of trying to make ends meet for these characters, there must have been the news, in the twenties, of this man preaching some kind of revolution, and I thought, of course, sometimes we want to be a part of that big Voice, we want to slip ourselves into history as a way to affirm our existence. Garvey must have given so many people this magical gift. The poem is in praise of such dangerous and sweetly affirming magic. Garvey has always been the pioneering of West Indian Americanness, for me. Garvey's life has been both an example and a lesson in how quickly xenophobia can canker embrace. This, too, is another kind of America."

JOEL DIAS-PORTER (aka DJ Renegade) was born in Pittsburgh, Pennsylvania, in 1962, and was raised there. He is a former professional DJ. He was the 1998 and '99 Haiku Slam Champion. In 1995, he received the Furious Flower "Emerging Poet Award." He appeared in the feature film *Slam Nation*. A Cave Canem fellow and the father of a young son, he has a CD of jazz and poetry entitled *LibationSong*.

Of "Elegy Indigo," Dias-Porter writes: "This poem includes a line from the song 'Open Heart' by Sekou Sundiata, a line that as much as I loved the song, I couldn't understand. It played over and over in my head, a haunting refrain. When Sekou suddenly passed it finally hit me in a kind of Zen flash, the line was a corollary of the old proverb 'You don't miss your water until the well runs dry.'"

NATALIE DIAZ was born in Needles, California, in September 1978. She is director of the Fort Mojave Language Recovery Program, where she works and teaches with the last speakers of the Mojave language. She played professional basketball in Europe and Asia after playing Division I basketball for Old Dominion University. She is a Lannan Fellow and teaches at the Institute of American Indian Arts low-residency MFA program in Santa Fe, New Mexico. She lives in Mohave Valley, Arizona.

Of "These Hands, if Not Gods," Diaz writes: "The images and hands of this poem began building during Mass one Sunday. The reading was about the laying of hands on someone, and I began thinking of how my own hands work upon a body. How they do things both beautiful and awful—to trace a throat gently in one moment, to hold it tightly in another—a type of sweet wreckery that makes me feel godlike and helpless all at once."

MARK DOTY was born in Maryville, Tennessee, in 1953. His nine books of poems include *Fire to Fire: New and Selected Poems* (HarperCollins, 2008), which won the National Book Award for poetry, and, most recently, *A Swarm, A Flock, A Host: A Compendium of Creatures* (Prestel,

2013), a collaboration with the painter Darren Waterston. He is also the author of five volumes of nonfiction prose, most recently *The Art of Description: World into Word* (Graywolf, 2010). A distinguished professor at Rutgers University, he lives in New York City and on the east end of Long Island. "Deep Lane" is the title poem of his new collection, which W. W. Norton will publish in 2015. He was the guest editor of *The Best American Poetry 2012.*

Doty writes: "Deep Lane is a real road, in Amagansett, New York, a beautiful one, but in truth it's the name I love: the two monosyllables, the two long vowels, the sense of going forward and down at once, descending into . . . what? Five years ago, when I began to tend a home and garden a couple of miles away from Deep Lane, that name began to draw associations toward itself, a magnet gathering bits of psychic metal; 'Deep Lane' came to suggest for me a kind of visionary pull toward the subterranean, the underworld, the life concealed beneath this one. I wrote a poem called 'Deep Lane,' but as soon as I was done I knew there was more for me to investigate in that phrase, more than I'd foreseen. At the very back of my garden is the tail end of the Ronkonkoma Moraine, a ridge of earth pushed up by the last Ice Age glacier 10,000 years ago. My narrow bit of land rises perhaps a dozen feet, just enough to create a sense of mystery, and when the wind blows down in it, sometimes I'm not sure when and where that wind is from. This poem wants to consider the idea that it's the wind blowing out of Nowhere, the wind of the grave, and perhaps we could take pleasure in the energizing possibility of being no one, giving ourselves over to a free, wild shape-shifting wind. What might be gained from the self having no border, and what lost?"

SEAN THOMAS DOUGHERTY was born in New York City in 1965. He was raised in Toledo, Ohio, and Manchester, New Hampshire, with many summers spent in Portland, Maine. As an adult he has lived in Syracuse, New York, and Cleveland, Ohio, and for more than a decade on and off in Erie, Pennsylvania. He is the author or editor of thirteen books. They include *All You Ask for Is Longing: New and Selected Poems (BOA Editions, 2014)*; *Scything Grace* (Etruscan Press, 2013); *Sasha Sings the Laundry on the Line* (BOA Editions, 2010), which was a finalist for Binghamton University's Milton Kessler literary prize for the best book by a poet over forty; the novella *The Blue City* (Marick Press/Wayne State University, 2008); and *Broken Hallelujahs* (BOA Editions, 2007). He has won two Pennsylvania Council for the Arts Fellowships in Poetry and a Fulbright Lectureship to the Balkans. He works at a pool hall and teaches private students.

On "The Blues Is a Verb," Dougherty writes: "Most of my work is fueled by despair, loss, and disjunction. But it also exhibits the defiance not to die that I have embraced—as have many friends, despite loss of jobs and other setbacks. We enact the Blues, the poem says. It moves, it darts, it jabs. I can locate the poem's emotional origins and landscape in two urban areas where I've lived: in the east side of Erie, Pennsylvania, and the east side of Cleveland, Ohio, where I used to wander, drink, and shoot pool. Some lines come straight from these neighborhoods. Mrs. Janofsky, my neighbor, with her wasted son. My wanderings at night, walking everywhere, a cue on my back. Playing men for money in bars, the gaze in my eyes that said, *don't*. Often we ended up laughing, talking of music and sports and our women. I lost more than enough to keep everyone laughing. The anger from all the years of losses unraveled slowly. The poem's last line owes its origin to watching my sick girlfriend's mother scratch a lottery ticket. All of us scratching lottery tickets, bottling up change. The drugs that I've seen take too many. This is the America for most of us, which too often doesn't make it into American poetry: hence the riff on Eliot. There is nothing romantic here, except survival. No one is coming to save us but ourselves. And besides, even if we have nothing, we have our voices, bitterly fierce; we have our verbs."

RITA DOVE is a former United States Poet Laureate (1993–1995) and recipient of the 1987 Pulitzer Prize in poetry for *Thomas and Beulah* (Carnegie Mellon University Press). Born in Akron, Ohio, in 1952, she is the author of nine poetry collections, most recently *Sonata Mulattica* (2009) and *American Smooth* (2004)—both from W. W. Norton & Company, as well as a collection of short stories, a novel, and a play. She edited *The Penguin Anthology of Twentieth-Century American Poetry* (2011). She has received numerous honors, among them twenty-four honorary doctorates, the 1996 National Humanities Medal from President Clinton, and the 2011 National Medal of Arts from President Obama, the only poet to have both medals to her credit. She is Commonwealth Professor of English at the University of Virginia. She was the guest editor of *The Best American Poetry 2000*.

CAMILLE DUNGY was born in Denver, Colorado, in 1972, moved away two years later, and proceeded to live in eight different cities before returning to Colorado with her husband and daughter in 2013. She is the author of three books of poetry: *Smith Blue* (2011), *Suck on the Marrow* (2010), and *What to Eat, What to Drink, What to Leave for Poison* (2006). She edited *Black Nature: Four Centuries of African American Nature Poetry* (2009) and coedited *From the Fishhouse: An Anthology of Poems that Sing, Rhyme, Resound, Syncopate, Alliterate, and Just Plain Sound Great* (2009). She has served as assistant editor for *Gathering Ground: A Reader Celebrating Cave Canem's First Decade* (2006). Her honors include an American Book Award, two Northern California Book Awards, a California Book Award silver medal, two NAACP Image Award nominations, a fellowship from the National Endowment for the Arts, and a fellowship from the Sustainable Arts Foundation. She now teaches English at Colorado State University in Fort Collins.

Of "Conspiracy (to breathe together)," Dungy writes: "Pieces of this poem come from many experiences, and each of them is true, though none is the complete truth. I keep notes on my experiences and my reactions to them, and I've learned to be patient about selecting how to use these notes. When my friend the Reverend Jack Shriver gave the etymology of the word 'conspiracy' one Sunday, he reminded me that the negative connotations we give the word need not be the only possibilities for understanding the act of breathing together. I realized, then, that I had discovered the glue I needed to connect some of my disparate notes. Of course, as I drafted the poem, even more revealed itself to me. That's the beauty of poetry."

Born in 1954, CORNELIUS EADY was raised in Rochester, New York. He attended Monroe Community College and Empire State College. He is the author of *Hardheaded Weather* (G. P. Putnam's Sons, 2008); *Brutal Imagination* (2001); *the autobiography of a jukebox* (1997); *You Don't Miss Your Water* (1995); *The Gathering of My Name* (1991); *BOOM BOOM BOOM* (1988); *Victims of the Latest Dance Craze* (1985), which won the 1985 Lamont Poetry Selection of the Academy of American Poets; and *Kartunes* (1980). In 1996, Eady and Toi Derricotte founded Cave Canem, a nonprofit organization serving black poets of various backgrounds and acting as a safe space for intellectual engagement and critical debate. Along with Derricotte, he edited *Gathering Ground* (University of Michigan Press, 2006). He has collaborated with jazz composer Deidre Murray in the production of several works of musical theater, including *You Don't Miss Your Water*, *Fangs*, and *Brutal Imagination*. He has won a Lila Wallace–Reader's Digest Writers Award and fellowships from the Guggenheim Foundation, the National Endowment for the Arts, and the Rockefeller Foundation. He holds the Miller Chair in Poetry at the University of Missouri.

VIEVEE FRANCIS was born in San Angelo, Texas, in 1963. She considers herself permanently at home in the Detroit metropolitan area, where she has lived off and on for three decades. She is the author of two poetry collections, *Blue-Tail Fly* (Wayne State University Press, 2006) and *Horse in the Dark*, winner of the Cave Canem Northwestern University Press Prize for a second book (Northwestern University Press, 2012). She won a 2009 Rona Jaffe Award, a 2010 Kresge Artist Fellowship, and a 2013 Bread Loaf Fellowship. She is an associate editor for *Callaloo* and a visiting professor of creative writing at Warren Wilson College in the mountains of Western North Carolina.

Of "Fallen," Francis writes: "My work often explores the ways in which we are limited or reduced by received notions concerning aesthetics. The frames we deny we are in or fear breaking even when we are aware of them. 'Fallen' ultimately rose from my own longing to be 'seen' on my own terms, not those of family/clan or culture. It begins a personal exploration of the *various* ways one might be rendered invisible. What is 'ugly'? Why? What does it mean to be a daughter outside of the framework/s of Beauty? What does it mean to be a poet who is a woman but is neither muse nor maternal, and does not seek such currency, but feels the loss and bears the indignities of not having such currency?"

ROSS GAY was born in Youngstown, Ohio, in 1974. He teaches creative writing at Indiana University in Bloomington. He is the author of *Against Which* (CavanKerry, 2006) and *Bringing the Shovel Down* (University of Pittsburgh Press, 2011), and coauthor, with Aimee Nezhukumatathil, of the chapbook *Lace and Pyrite: Letters from Two Gardens* (Organic Weapon Arts, 2014). He is an editor with the chapbook press Q Avenue and an editor and cofounder, with Patrick Rosal, of the online sports magazine *Some Call It Ballin'*. He is a 2013 Guggenheim Fellow.

Of "To the Fig Tree on 9th and Christian," Gay writes: "This poem was, more or less, given to me by the event I tell about, most of which, give or take, happened on a beautiful day in early fall, when this particular variety of fig (I'd speculate either a Brown Turkey or Chicago Hardy, given the color of the flesh and the hardiness) was ripening. I was on my way to eat breakfast alone at Sabrina's, a damn good restaurant right across Christian Street (vegetarian cheese-steak hold the cheese, and French fries, best in town). I was stuck, as I often am, in my head. And on my way I noticed this woman sweeping the sidewalk, sweating some, half cursing her work, though smiling, too, and shaking her head, as if to say, 'Can you believe this thing?' and actually saying, 'Please eat some,' pointing up into the tree and down at the sidewalk. And, just as in the poem, soon enough there was a little gathering of strangers, mild-mannered yellow jackets included, shooting the breeze about figs ('growing all the way up here?!'), getting on our tippy toes to pick them and pass them around, all of us making the noises of people enjoying food together, which are close cousins to other noises, you know.

"I've been lucky enough to work with a public community orchard in Bloomington, Indiana, where I teach, for the last few years. We have planted nearly one hundred trees, and part of the magic of the project is knowing that, if all goes well, people you can't have imagined will eat fruit from trees you helped plant. We have a fig tree at the Bloomington Community Orchard, too, and it's about my height, and came from a cutting from the man I mention in the poem, a dear friend's father, who gave me my first fresh figs. He dug it up kind of roughly with a hoe and threw it in a bucket of water. 'Keep it wet,' is all he said, and made a motion with his hand that seemed to mean something like, 'Now scram.' That wet stick made it to Indiana and became a tree. Now people come to the orchard and gasp when they see we have figs, and they faint when they eat them, especially if they're sun-warmed. We keep smelling salts and lavender water in a spray bottle for when it happens, which is more often than you'd think. I love to imagine my friend's father seeing us savoring those figs, seeing the way something he nurtured makes us glad, makes us stand in a circle and listen to one another. Much as I like to imagine whoever planted that tree on 9th and Christian listening to us, or watching."

EUGENE GLORIA was born in Manila, Philippines, in 1957. His family immigrated to San Francisco, California, when he was eight years old. He earned an undergraduate degree at San Francisco State University and graduate degrees at Miami University of Ohio and the University of Oregon. He now lives in Greencastle, Indiana, where he is a professor of English literature and creative writing at DePauw University. He was recently the Arts and Sciences Distinguished Visiting Writer at

Bowling Green State University in Ohio. He is the author of *Drivers at the Short-Time Motel* (Penguin Books, 2000), *Hoodlum Birds* (Penguin, 2006), and *My Favorite Warlord* (Penguin, 2012), which was awarded the Anisfield-Wolf Book Award for poetry in 2013.

Of "Liner Notes for Monk," Gloria writes: "For those in the post-vinyl era, 'liner notes' were mini essays on the origins of the music and some background material on the musicians, usually written by the album's producer and printed on the album's back cover. As for the 'liner notes' on my poem, I drew inspiration in part from the legendary Riverside Recordings of Thelonius Monk with John Coltrane in 1957, but more from Eddie Jefferson and what he's done by singing his own lyrics to such iconic instrumental classics as 'Body and Soul' by Coleman Hawkins and 'So What' by Miles Davis. While I was working on this poem, I was finishing *My Favorite Warlord*, a collection of poems exploring, among other things, the haibun, a hybrid form linking travel sketches and the haiku, a form invented by the great Buddhist monk poet, Bashō. So in some way, 'the lyrics' I devised were personal travel sketches from my time living in Kyoto. Thelonius Monk's music is easy to love, but not easy to explain. So I assumed the task of explaining his music to myself by way of recalling my solitary nights living in Kyoto several years ago."

RAY GONZALEZ was born in El Paso, Texas, in 1952. He is a professor of English in the MFA Program at the University of Minnesota in Minneapolis. He is the author of fourteen books of poetry, including six from BOA Editions, the most recent being *Cool Auditor* (2009) and the forthcoming *Beautiful Wall* (2015). He was awarded the Minnesota Book Award in poetry for *Turtle Pictures* (University of Arizona Press, 2000) and for *The Hawk Temple at Tierra Grande* (BOA, 2002). He has written three books of nonfiction, including *The Underground Heart: A Return to a Hidden Landscape* (Arizona, 2002). He has edited twelve anthologies and coedited *Sudden Fiction Latino* (W. W. Norton, 2010) with Robert Shapard and James Thomas. He received a 2004 Lifetime Achievement Award from the Southwest Border Regional Library Association.

Of "One El Paso, Two El Paso," Gonzalez writes: "The U.S.–Mexican border and its conflicts are in the news all the time, though, growing up in the El Paso–Juarez, Mexico area, I have always found peace and freedom in the vast and quiet landscapes of the Chihuahuan Desert. These mountains, canyons, and arroyos were key influences in my becoming a poet. While immigration has been an issue on the invisible border for generations, the area became one of the most dangerous in the world during the recent drug cartel wars across the Rio Grande in Juarez, Mexico. Ironically, El Paso was named the safest city in the United States from 2008 through 2010, proving my theory that there are two rival border narratives centering on two similar cities and ways of life, the two mountain ranges surrounding them, and the idea that one active poem comes from daily life and treks across the desert while the other mythical poem of the region's past lies somewhere under the historic dust of the desert. Each time I return to my hometown, the desert has changed, and each visit leads to a fresh source of often sobering inspiration."

KATHLEEN GRABER was born in Cape May Court House, New Jersey, in 1959. She is an associate professor of English at Virginia Commonwealth University. She is the author of two collections of poetry, *Correspondence* (Saturnalia Books, 2006) and *The Eternal City* (Princeton University Press, 2010), which was a finalist for the National Book Award. She has received fellowships from the National Endowment for the Arts and the Guggenheim Foundation.

Graber writes: "'The River Twice' takes its title from a fragment attributed to the Pre-Socratic philosopher Heraclitus: *No man can step into the same river twice, for it is not the same river and he is not the same man.* Heraclitus is perhaps the most alluring, complex, and mystical of the early Greek thinkers, and his assertion that both the world and our identities are in constant 'flux' seems shockingly contemporary. Constant change is, however, only one aspect of the system we see hinted at in the passages that have survived, for this fluid-like change is balanced against an originating fiery force he refers to as *logos*, a word that in Greek connotes both reason and language, a stroke of linguistic confluence not unworthy of Wittgenstein, Derrida, or Bertrand Russell.

"This poem, however, simply attempts to deliver an experience of how it feels to live in the destabilized modern world in which flux can be—as it has always been—dramatic and potentially deadly, and the figures in the poem have very little control over, or protection against, that which is changing economically and environmentally around them. There is also a little nod to Keats and the stasis art sometimes affords. Simultaneously, this is also a poem about many varieties of causality and agency and our fairly limited existential understanding of both. I think most of us inhabit a state of perpetual cognitive dissonance in which we posit that we are both responsible and not responsible for many of the defining circumstances of our lives. Most of us might accept that we have at least been unwitting contributors. The question of how much power we have over the powers that have power over us is largely unanswerable. It is, nevertheless, a question that informs our sense of our relationships to our governments, our financial institutions, our geographies, our bodies, our parents, and our gods. I did NOT sit down to write this poem thinking about any of this. I simply sat down to write about wandering around in a thrift store on a rainy day."

ROSEMARY GRIGGS was born in Oak Lawn, Illinois, in 1973. She received her BA from the University of Iowa and MFA from San Francisco State University. *Sky Girl*, her book of poems, won the 2003 Alberta Prize and was published by Fence Books. She supports herself working as a flight attendant, a job that permits her to meander the earth and encounter different cultures. She lives in Oakland, California.

On "SCRIPT POEM," Griggs writes: "I find the screenplay format poetic in its attention to imagery, spacing, and economy of words. This poem is about my mailman in San Francisco who was in the reserves and got called in for a tour of duty. I have never shared the poem with him but I will now and I think it's going to make him happy—which makes me happy. With filmmaker Tor Hansen and composer David Rhodes, I collaborated on a short film of one of my poems, which can be found at http://vimeo.com/48717613."

ADAM HAMMER was born in 1948 in New Jersey. He studied at Emerson College, the University of Massachusetts, the University of California Santa Barbara, Colorado State University, and Bowling Green State University, from which he received a PhD in popular culture. His books are *On a Train Sleeping* (Barn Dream Press/Pym-Randall Press, 1970), *Déjà Everything* (Lynx House Press, 1979), and *No Time for Dancing* (Willow Spring Editions, 2010, edited by Christopher Howell). With Yusef Komunyakaa, he was cofounder of the literary journal *Gumbo*, which he edited for several years in the late 1970s. He died in a head-on collision with a truck outside Pensacola, Florida, in 1984. He was, Christopher Howell writes in *Pleiades*, "six foot one and lanky, with a long jaw and a great mop of black hair that sometimes resembled dreadlocks. He was left-handed and, in spite of his frequent abuse of every substance worth abusing, was a fabulous ball player and could throw a marshmallow through a brick wall." He embraced French surrealism and wrote about subjects ranging from the death of Hubert Humphrey to nurses, intellectuals, hockey, Belgium, and Africa.

BOB HICOK's seventh book is *Elegy Owed* (Copper Canyon, 2013). He is the recipient of a Guggenheim and two NEA Fellowships, as well as the Bobbitt Prize from the Library of Congress. He lives in Virginia.

Of "Blue prints," Hicok writes: "A lot of things, once they happen, seem inevitable. Poems often feel like shapes that were there but unnoticed until touched. Love too—as soon as I saw the woman who'd become my wife, it seemed she'd always been there. Wouldn't it be weird if she had—if we'd been walking around sort of back to back without realizing, without turning toward the other? Cool scary. I hope builders don't think this poem is trying to put them out of work."

LE HINTON was born in Harrisburg, Pennsylvania, in 1952. He received his BA from Saint Joseph's College in Philadelphia and is currently the editor of the journal *Fledgling Rag*. He is the author of five collections of poetry: *Waiting for Brion* (2004), *Status Post Hope* (2006), *Black on Most Days* (2008), *The God of Our Dreams* (2010), and *The Language of Moisture and Light* (2014), all published by Iris G. Press. His poem "Our Ballpark" was incorporated into Derek Parker's sculpture *Common Thread* and installed at Clipper Magazine Stadium in Lancaster, Pennsylvania, where he has lived for the past thirty-one years.

Hinton writes: " 'No Doubt About It (I Gotta Get Another Hat)' is an elegy for the Baltimore poet Chris Toll and is infused with his spirit. As to the 'Vincent' in the poem's first line: in the 1960s the actor Vincent Price sold original art for Sears. For an assignment in high school, I wrote to him and asked, 'What is art?' It is a question I continue to ask."

TONY HOAGLAND was born in North Carolina in 1953. His books of poems include *What Narcissism Means to Me*, *Unincorporated Persons in the Late Honda Dynasty*, and *Donkey Gospel*. His work has received the Mark Twain Award, a Guggenheim Fellowship, and the Jackson Poetry Prize. His second book of prose essays, *Twenty Poems That Could Save America and Other Essays*, will be published by Graywolf Press in 2014. Several years ago he founded FivePowersPoetry.com, a short-form program for coaching high school teachers in the teaching of poetry in the classroom. He teaches creative writing at the University of Houston.

Of "Write Whiter," Hoagland writes: "Categories of perception are always shifting, shrinking, and expanding, and they are always reductive, and they are inevitable. That doesn't mean that they are comfortable. And what time-honored opportunities they have provided for malice, persecution, and control.

"To play with such categories, to mock and acknowledge them at the same time, is a mode of struggle, and a way of keeping clear of the traps they construct for us. The playful and iconoclastic deftness of poetry is meant for tasks like this. The soul can't be trapped, and yet it is. That paradox is the instinct from which this writing came. It's a lament, but it's also an anti-Prohibition poem. I don't consider 'Write Whiter' a great poem, nor an exceptional example of TH's volcanic talent. Someone else easily could have written it. However, it defines, like a station of the cross, a place in the conversation we are having; its ticket needed to be punched, and so I punched it."

MAJOR JACKSON is the author of three collections of poetry: *Holding Company*, *Hoops*, and *Leaving Saturn*. He is the editor of Library of America's *Countee Cullen: Collected Poems* and is a recipient of a Guggenheim Fellowship, Pushcart Prize, and a Whiting Writers' Award. A core faculty member of the Bennington Writing Seminars, he is the Richard A. Dennis University Professor at the University of Vermont. He divides his time between Florida and Vermont.

Of "OK Cupid," Jackson writes: "Lately, I have been fascinated with the tradition of American poems that create their own logic and systems of meaning, that are explicitly and deliberately constructed out of a strong sense of inventiveness, play, and chance, what some have been labeling 'procedural,' which also incidentally (and hilarious to me) described my series of 'dates' while I was briefly on a few online dating websites. Initially, I found the battery of questions designed to feed into an algorithm of answers that ostensibly would spit out an instant list of potential life partners absolutely appalling, even while I morosely answered every question to completeness. Putting my ire and pessimism aside, I commenced to writing a long poem using the generative phrase 'Dating a _____ is like dating a _____.' As each line came to me, mocking the whole enterprise of Internet matchmaking, I loved the associative spirit of what was emerging as well as the freedom to go wherever I wanted, which was unlike the word analogy problems my middle school teacher doled out, that seemed fixed, easily formulated, and too logical. The poem started as a parody and critique of the social order, but emerged with greater aesthetic outcomes: whimsy and flight. The poem contracts between the uproarious and the serious. It turned out my subconscious didn't want to condemn dating websites after all, but to simply have fun. And thus, I now regret having written the disclaimer that is published with my biography in *Tin House*."

AMAUD JAMAUL JOHNSON was born in Compton, California, in 1972. Educated at Howard University and Cornell University, he is the author of two poetry collections, *Darktown Follies* (Tupelo Press, 2013) and *Red Summer* (Tupelo, 2006), which Carl Phillips selected as winner of the Dorset Prize. A former Wallace Stegner Fellow in poetry at Stanford, a Robert Frost Fellow at the Bread Loaf Writers' Conference, and a Cave Canem Fellow, he teaches in the MFA Program in creative writing at the University of Wisconsin-Madison.

Of "L.A. Police Chief Daryl Gates Dead at 83," Johnson writes: "Los Angeles in the mid-1980s seemed near-apocalyptic. There was fire and brimstone in the pulpit, addiction, gang violence, and police brutality on the corner, and nuclear war on the screen. Magic Johnson deserved a Nobel Peace Prize for his 'no look alley-oop,' because without the Lakers, the city might have burned five years before the 1992 riots. I happened across the headline of Daryl Gates's passing a few years ago, and I was caught off guard by my emotional response. I wanted to blame him for all the evils of that decade. Of course, blaming the dead is a form of failure. The dead are defenseless. The dead can't plead forgiveness. Punishment and pity are tools for the living."

DOUGLAS KEARNEY is a poet, performer, and librettist. His second full-length collection of poetry, *The Black Automaton* (Fence Books, 2009), was Catherine Wagner's selection for the National Poetry Series. Red Hen Press published Kearney's third collection, *Patter*, in 2014. He has received fellowships at Cave Canem, Idyllwild, and elsewhere. His work has appeared in a number of journals, including *Poetry*, *nocturnes*, *Pleiades*, *Callaloo*, *Ninth Letter*. His produced operas include *Sucktion*, *Mordake*, and *Crescent City*. Raised in Altadena, California, he lives with his family in California's Santa Clarita Valley. He teaches at CalArts, where he received his MFA in Writing in 2004.

Of "The Labor of Stagger Lee: Boar," Kearney writes: "I tend to be series-oriented in my writing. Having the time and space to develop a number of ideas and images around a central one allows me to unsettle my own expectations around what poems can yield. For several years, I wanted to work with the Labors of Herakles. It would be great: there were twelve, so I had a positive constraint for, say, a twelve-poem series. But I never figured out a useful entry point for trotting out some more Greek mythology.

"Then, the saloon doors opened and in walked Stagger Lee.

"It occurred to me that I could take these two infamous badmen—

Stagger and Herakles—and conflate them somehow. Both versions say interesting things to their respective cultures about the nature of violence, suffering, and the heroic. Thus, acting like some new jack Eurystheus, I sent Stagger Lee on his own version of Herakles' labors. Of course, Herakles took on his work—many say—because he killed his family. The work Stagger puts in, in my series, *is* the killing of his 'brother' (see the language of Black uplift), Billy Lyons.

"In 'The Labor of Stagger Lee: Boar,' we see Stagger and a fractalized kind of Erymanthian Boar. Yet, as is the case in the labors of antiquity, the pig can come to signify some culturally specific notions. I think they're apparent here.

"Oh! Last thing. At one point, this poem was, itself, divided into two sections. 'Rooter' and 'Tooter'—a nod to an old expression about how much of the hog hungry black folks would eat. The 'Tooter' section lost track of Stagger completely and started riffing on Herakles and 'That Scene' from *Deliverance*. It was a jazz to write, but it jumped the shark. Utterly. I had clutched to it, unwilling to admit it wasn't working. A chat with poet Jericho Brown helped cinch its excision."

YUSEF KOMUNYAKAA'S books of poetry include *Taboo*, *Dien Cai Dau*, *Neon Vernacular* (for which he received the Pulitzer Prize), *The Chameleon Couch*, and *Testimony: A Tribute to Charlie Parker*. He has received numerous awards, including the William Faulkner Prize (Université de Rennes, France), the Kingsley Tufts Award for Poetry, the Ruth Lilly Poetry Prize, and the 2011 Wallace Stevens Award. His plays, performance art, and libretti have been performed internationally, and include *Slipknot*, *Wakonda's Dream*, *Nine Bridges Back*, *Saturnalia*, *Testimony*, *The Mercy Suite*, and *Gilgamesh: A Verse Play* (with Chad Gracia). He teaches at New York University. He was the guest editor of *The Best American Poetry 2003*.

Komunyakaa writes: " 'Negritude' is an improvised meditation on the term. In *Cahier d'un retour au pays natal* (1939), Aimé Césaire defines negritude as 'the simple recognition of the fact that one is black, the acceptance of this fact and of our destiny as blacks, of our history and culture.' It was, however, Wole Soyinka who said, 'A tiger doesn't proclaim its tigerness; it jumps on its prey.'

"Perhaps this poem, through a composite of images, underscores these vagaries within a state of being; perhaps we are, intellectually and spiritually, the summation of the inherited metaphors we can't help but live by. The speaker seems to have been shaped by the basic rituals of earthy existence—the blues, hard work, dance, folklore, love, time, nature, and even gratitude; the sum total of his life has been a full-blown beckoning and a reckoning. This poem—in celebration of Césaire's centennial—challenges his definition by suggesting that 'negritude' is not a decision, but a condition of the soul."

HAILEY LEITHAUSER was born in Baltimore, Maryland, in 1954. She is the author of *Swoop*, which was published by Graywolf in 2013. Her work was selected for *The Best American Poetry 2010*. She teaches at the Writer's Center in Bethesda, Maryland.

Of "In My Last Past Life," Leithauser writes: "I don't remember much about how I came to write this poem except that the first line was buzzing around in my brain for several years, and that I always thought of it as a good line to open a villanelle. I do remember that I tried a few times to write it as a sort of humorous fairy tale, but those attempts never quite fell into place. It wasn't until this last version, when the sea began returning in each stanza, that the poem developed the elegiac tone that was apparently the speaker's proper voice."

LARRY LEVIS (1946–1996) published five collections of poetry during his lifetime. *Elegy*, a posthumous volume edited by Philip Levine, appeared in 1997, and *Selected Levis*, edited by David St. John, was published in 2000.

David St. John writes: " 'Elegy with a Darkening Trapeze inside It' is, in effect, the title poem of Larry Levis's *The Darkening Trapeze: The Uncollected Poems of Larry Levis*, forthcoming from Graywolf Press, which I edited. These 'last' poems were written almost entirely during the same time frame as those in his posthumous book, *Elegy* (1997). Many of the poems are longer, even operatic pieces that reflect Larry's dramatic—and elaborate—narrative braiding, which became the poetic signature for much of his later work. Larry Levis died in May 1996, and what *The Darkening Trapeze* makes clear is that his poetry remains some of the most lyrically complex and consistently powerful work being published in this country."

GARY COPELAND LILLEY, a North Carolina native, lives and teaches in Winston-Salem. He received the 1996 and 2000 DC Commission for the Arts Fellowship for Poetry, and earned his MFA from the Warren Wilson College Program for Writers. He is a member of the Black Rooster Collective, is a Cave Canem fellow, and has taught in the undergraduate writing program at Warren Wilson College, and in the

Great Smokies writing program at the University of North Carolina-Asheville. He has been a faculty poet at the Port Townsend Writers Conference and a visiting writer at Colby College, the University of Arizona, Goddard College, and the Institute of American Indian Art. His books include *High Water Everywhere* (Willow Books of Aquarius Press, 2013), *Alpha Zulu* (Ausable Press, 2008), and *The Subsequent Blues* (Four Way Books, 2004).

Of "Sermon of the Dreadnaught," Lilley writes: "I love the blues, and blues people. They've always been around me, and a few years ago a friend put a guitar in my hands. I play every day, both secular and sacred blues. I am a devotee, most happy when I am creating music and fueling my writing. I play on the streets in small towns, cities, churches, bars, and homes of inviting folks. I wanted this poem to capture some of that energy, some of the deep resonance of the dreadnaught-style acoustic guitar, and some images of the blues-people terrain. And yes, there were tunes running through my head when I was developing the poem. Old-time gospel songs that are starting to disappear even from the song lists of black churches, the songs of my grandmothers, and all the old people from the rural North Carolina community in which I grew up. I call them foundation songs. That dreadnaught guitar brought those songs back to me, and gave me the poem."

Frannie Lindsay was born in Princeton, New Jersey, in 1949. Her four volumes of poetry are *Our Vanishing* (Red Hen Press, 2014), *Mayweed* (The Word Works, 2010), *Lamb* (Perugia Press, 2006), and *Where She Always Was* (Utah State University Press, 2004). She has won the Benjamin Saltman Award, the Washington Prize, the Perugia Prize, and the May Swenson Award. In 2008 she was chosen as the winner of *The Missouri Review* Prize in poetry. She has held fellowships from the National Endowment for the Arts and the Massachusetts Cultural Council. She is also a classical pianist. Over the last twenty years, she has rescued seven greyhounds. She lives near Boston, Massachusetts.

Of "Elegy for My Mother," Lindsay writes: "I write many of my best poems in what I think of as a state of ecstasy. This, certainly, is far from unique among poets. Ecstatic pieces tend to announce their arrival at times when the act of writing is utterly inconvenient: in the shower, walking the dog, any circumstance in which I am without paper and pen. 'Elegy for My Mother' is one of these. I have only a few minutes to capture these poems, and getting them down requires nothing short of blind trust. I don't have time to question a word, a phrase, or a line.

I have to write fast. I often abbreviate words or scribbled graphic symbols. Usually, I revise them only a little or not at all.

"In order to write this way, one has to listen, surrender, and then just plain take dictation. The lines and images may be overtly relevant to one another or not (often the less relevant, the better). What binds them at first is merely the speed and certainty with which they arrive, and sometimes this remains the primary commonality; sometimes this connective tissue was nothing more than filaments. So much the better: the writer is left with a poem that is illuminated by just the right madness."

PATRICIA LOCKWOOD was born in a trailer in Fort Wayne, Indiana, in 1982, and grew up in all the worst cities of the Midwest. She is the author of the poetry collections *Balloon Pop Outlaw Black* (Octopus Books, 2012) and *Motherland Fatherland Homelandsexuals* (Penguin Books, 2014).

Lockwood writes: "I wrote 'Rape Joke' because I wanted to know if it was possible. (Most poems are not possible, and this one seemed even less possible than usual.) When the conceit presented itself to me, I saw that if I did it correctly, I could write a poem that was personal, true, appalling, and even occasionally funny. If I did it correctly, it would speak straight out of the mouth of the event but still be recognizable as a poem. It seemed like a high-wire act. I wanted to know if I could do it."

NATHANIEL MACKEY was born in Miami, Florida, in 1947, and grew up, from age four, in California. He is the author of five books of poetry, the most recent of which are *Splay Anthem* (New Directions, 2006) and *Nod House* (New Directions, 2011); an ongoing prose work, *From a Broken Bottle Traces of Perfume Still Emanate*, whose fourth and most recent volume is *Bass Cathedral* (New Directions, 2008) and whose first three volumes have been published together as *From a Broken Bottle Traces of Perfume Still Emanate: Volumes 1–3* (New Directions, 2010); and two books of criticism, the most recent of which is *Paracritical Hinge: Essays, Talks, Notes, Interviews* (University of Wisconsin Press, 2005). He is the editor of the literary magazine *Hambone* and coeditor, with Art Lange, of the anthology *Moment's Notice: Jazz in Poetry and Prose* (Coffee House Press, 1993). He received a Whiting Writers' Award in 1993, was elected to the Board of Chancellors of the Academy of American Poets in 2001, won the National Book Award in poetry for *Splay Anthem* in 2006 and a Guggenheim Fellowship in 2010. He lives in Durham, North Carolina, and teaches at Duke University.

CATE MARVIN was born in Washington, DC, in 1969. She is a professor of English at the College of Staten Island, City University of New York, where she has taught creative writing since 2003. *World's Tallest Disaster* (2001), her first book, was selected by Robert Pinsky for Sarabande Books' Kathryn A. Morton Prize, and went on to receive the 2002 Kate Tufts Discovery Award. She is coeditor with poet Michael Dumanis of the anthology *Legitimate Dangers: American Poets of the New Century* (Sarabande, 2006). Her second book of poems, *Fragment of the Head of a Queen*, appeared from Sarabande in 2007. A Whiting Award recipient, Marvin has a third book of poems, *Oracle*, forthcoming from W. W. Norton in 2015. She is a cofounder, with Erin Belieu, of VIDA: Women in Literary Arts, a nonprofit organization that seeks to explore critical and cultural perceptions of writing by women.

Of "An Etiquette for Eyes," Marvin writes: "I like to think the voice of this poem goes off the rails in a manner similar to that of the French Surrealist poet Louis Aragon in his 'Poem to Shout in the Ruins.' Ultimately, 'An Etiquette for Eyes' advocates for the plain. Anyone with brown eyes knows the drill. The majority of people the world over have brown eyes, yet there exists an insufferable number of people with 'blue,' 'green,' and 'hazel' eyes who love to elaborate upon the changeability of the varying colors, hues, and shades of their respective irises. Being on the listening end of this species of self-appraisal can be pretty tedious when one's own eyes can only be described as 'brown.' In this sense, 'An Etiquette for Eyes' is quite simple. It's an argument for being ordinary, launched against an individual the poem's speaker once regarded as extraordinary."

JAMAAL MAY was born in 1982 in Detroit, Michigan, where he has taught poetry in public schools and worked as a freelance audio engineer and touring performer. His first book, *Hum*, received the Beatrice Hawley Award from Alice James Books. He teaches in the Vermont College of Fine Arts MFA program.

Of "Masticated Light," May writes: "When I was a member of the 2012 NYC louderARTS Poetry Slam Team I wrote a collaborative poem with a young poet named Mokgethi Thinane. We told stories to each other until several bridges were welded between us. Turns out we both have screwed-up eyes and that led to a poem about sight in its various meanings and registers. After the National Poetry Slam concluded, I sat with the pieces of the poem that were mine and was pleasantly disturbed by some of what was there. Working through the subject matter alongside Mokgethi had allowed me to tap into something I couldn't reach on my own. The difficulty of collaboration as a framework, combined with my terror of it, contributed to what broke me open. With those pieces to start with, I constructed the last poem to be added to *Hum*."

SHARA MCCALLUM was born in Kingston, Jamaica, in 1972. She is the author of four books: *The Face of Water: New and Selected Poems* (Peepal Tree Press, UK, 2011); *This Strange Land* (Alice James Books, 2011); *Song of Thieves* (University of Pittsburgh Press, 2003); and *The Water Between Us* (University of Pittsburgh Press, 1999), which won the 1998 Agnes Lynch Starrett Prize for Poetry. She received the 2013 Witter Bynner Fellowship. She is director of the Stadler Center for Poetry and professor of English at Bucknell University in Lewisburg, Pennsylvania.

McCallum writes: "In 'Parasol,' images from childhood and fairy tales led me to mull over the idea that metaphor, storytelling, and memory are entwined. They seem to be ways we can suspend and widen time in order to revisit other moments and selves we've been. This process is an act of the imagination, not the same as lived experience, and the poem registers the paradox that what might 'console' us is often that which we cannot hold onto. Poems about the past run the risk of becoming sentimental. At the time I wrote this poem I didn't consider point of view consciously. Now, on looking at it again, I imagine that the direct address to a 'you,' who I think is fairly obviously the poet-speaker, might also create a distance between speaker and subject that complicates the tone, helping the poem avoid diving headfirst into nostalgia.

"Lastly, rhyme played a significant part in the writing of this poem. I like to write from my ear, and with 'Parasol' associations of sound were particularly instructive, directing several turns and guiding the poem's insights."

MARTY MCCONNELL was born in Boston, Massachusetts, in 1973. She currently resides in Chicago, Illinois, where she works in fundraising and strategic planning for a youth and family center. Her first full-length collection, *wine for a shotgun*, was published in 2012 by EM Press. She cofounded the louderARTS Project in New York City and returned to Chicago in 2009 to create Vox Ferus, an organization dedicated to connecting individuals and communities through the written and spoken word.

Of "vivisection (you're going to break my heart)," McConnell writes: "I'm forever in pursuit of never writing another break-up poem, and here it is in *Best American*: a break-up poem. Appropriate, then, that this poem should actually deal with that very thing: the desire to be done with love and heartache, and the knowledge that given my nature, I'm unlikely ever to be done with it entirely. My first year in high school, we had to dissect a frog, and often when I am split open painfully by love, what flashes across my interior vision is that image, a creature so neatly dead and arrayed to be educational, useful, purposed. The whole thing is so delicate and gruesome, and simultaneously so absolutely ordinary."

VALZHYNA MORT was born in Minsk, Belarus (then part of the former Soviet Union), in 1981. She moved to the United States in 2005. Her two American collections, both published by Copper Canyon Press, are *Factory of Tears* (2008) and *Collected Body* (2011). She has received a Lannan Foundation Fellowship and the Bess Hokin Prize from *Poetry*. She is a visiting assistant professor at Cornell University.

Of "Sylt I," Mort writes: "This poem was written on the island of Sylt, in the North of Germany, a two-hour boat ride south of Copenhagen. Sylt has been a nudist destination for decades."

HARRYETTE MULLEN'S poetry collections include *Recyclopedia* (Graywolf Press, 2006), winner of a PEN Beyond Margins Award, and *Sleeping with the Dictionary* (University of California Press, 2002). She teaches American poetry, African American literature, and creative writing at UCLA. A collection of her essays and interviews, *The Cracks Between What We Are and What We Are Supposed to Be*, was published in 2012 by University of Alabama Press. Her most recent poetry collection, *Urban Tumbleweed: Notes from a Tanka Diary*, was published by Graywolf Press in 2013.

Of "Selection from Tanka Diary," Mullen wrote in the *Harvard Review*: "My tanka diary began with a wish to incorporate into my life a daily practice of walking and writing poetry. Usually I go for short walks in various parts of Los Angeles, Venice, and Santa Monica, or longer hikes in the canyons with friends. I also regularly lead student poets on 'tanka walks' in the Mildred Mathias Botanical Garden on the campus of UCLA. At other times I stroll through unfamiliar neighborhoods as I travel. These poems are my adaptation of a traditional Japanese form of syllabic poetry. Usually a tanka is thirty-one syllables, often written in five lines."

Asked to elaborate, Mullen adds the following under the heading "Urban Tumbleweed & the spirit of tanka": "The spirit of tanka interests me more than following rigid conventions. Succeeding generations rediscover and renew the form so that it retains its vitality. With *Urban Tumbleweed: Notes from a Tanka Diary*, my intention was not to write waka in a different language, not to replicate Japanese tanka, or translate the technicalities of that traditional form into a language with a different structure. Tanka is well suited for diary writing. It's a concise and efficient form of creative note-taking for sharpening daily observation and capturing the fleeting moment.

"I wanted to be attentive to moments that usually pass without notice. I wanted to preserve a fragment of each day. I was interested in what might be unique or idiosyncratic, but also in what is cyclical and what might be timeless.

"My aim for this project was to get myself moving. Tying the act of writing to a daily habit of walking was the impetus for this project. It gave me a little push to get past my inertia, to start the momentum of walking and writing.

"To walk in Los Angeles is to go against the way the city is constructed, with long blocks and wide streets built for cars and drivers, not pedestrians. Yet there are wonderful places for walking, on the beaches, in the canyons, and in neighborhoods where yards are planted with roses, lavender, hibiscus, and bird-of-paradise blooming year-round, along with abundant avocado, lemon, persimmon, apricot, and fig trees. Even the freeways are landscaped with oleander and bougainvillea."

Eileen Myles was born in Cambridge, Massachusetts, in December 1949, and generally occupies herself by writing and traveling and sometimes teaching at NYU and Columbia. She is the author of eighteen books of poetry (most recently *Snowflake/different streets* from Wave Books, 2012), fiction, and nonfiction.

Myles writes: "Certainly this poem was born at dinner when we were talking about conditions in the building we were dining in and the social ecology of women who could probably practically hear us talking about them. There was a painter who could pretty much lift any painting style; do anything. Thus the title, which seemed like a really generous way she could use her super powers. I think I also read about a famous male author who didn't like to hear about dreams at breakfast. What else is breakfast for? I definitely feel like this poem is about relatedness. In time *and* space."

D. NURKSE was born in New York City in 1949. He is the author of ten books of poetry, most recently *A Night in Brooklyn*, *The Border Kingdom*, *Burnt Island*, and *The Fall* (Alfred A. Knopf, 2012, 2008, 2005, and 2002). *Voices over Water*, an earlier book, was reprinted by CB Editions in the United Kingdom and shortlisted for the 2011 Forward Prize. He has received a literature award from the American Academy of Arts and Letters, a Guggenheim Fellowship, a Whiting Writers' Award, and fellowships from the National Endowment for the Arts and the New York Foundation for the Arts. He lives with his wife in Brooklyn and teaches at Sarah Lawrence College.

Of "Release from Stella Maris," Nurkse writes: "Soul, ego, neural network, illusion? I'm the person who reads the first hundred pages of a book on neuroscience or theology, then skips to the last ten. The answers must be in the middle. I'm comfortable being clueless. But the years roll."

SHARON OLDS is the author of nine books of poetry, including *The Dead and the Living*, which received the National Book Critics Circle Award, and *Stag's Leap* (Alfred A. Knopf, 2012), which won both the T. S. Eliot Prize and the Pulitzer Prize. She teaches at New York University's Graduate Program in Creative Writing, where she has been involved with NYU's outreach workshops, including the Goldwater Hospital workshop, in its twenty-eighth year, and the workshop for veterans of Iraq and Afghanistan.

Of "Stanley Kunitz Ode," Olds writes: "When I visited Stanley, I would go home and write down in my diary what had happened, what he had said, how he had looked. I was storing up Stanley memories. Years before, with Muriel Rukeyser, and George and Mary Oppen, I had done the same thing—always in prose. But on this particular day, after I wrote the first five words, it had the feeling of a poem, ready to shape itself, gathering itself around the totem creature of the bobcat. So (with pen and ink) I moved the words out of paragraph position, over to the left margin, and we were off. And as I just read it over, I noticed more than usually the four-accent Anglo Saxon line—the old story line. Whatever Stanley said and did had such a glow of significance, my wish was to try to transpose it whole into a narrative poem form."

GREGORY PARDLO was born in Philadelphia in 1968 and raised in Willingboro, New Jersey. He is the author of *Totem* (2007), which received *The American Poetry Review/* Honickman Prize, and *Digest* (Four Way

Books, 2014). He has received a New York Foundation for the Arts Fellowship and a fellowship for translation from the National Endowment for the Arts. He is an associate editor of *Callaloo* and teaches undergraduate writing at Columbia University.

Pardlo writes: " 'Wishing Well' is a true, which is to say, 'New York,' story."

KIKI PETROSINO (b. 1979 in Baltimore) is an assistant professor of English at the University of Louisville. She has written two poetry collections: *Fort Red Border* (2009) and *Hymn for the Black Terrific* (2013), both from Sarabande. She holds an MA in humanities from the University of Chicago and an MFA in creative writing from the University of Iowa Writers' Workshop.

Petrosino writes: "My poem 'Story Problem' came from an assignment I gave myself: to compose a poem that sounds logical but doesn't really know where it's going. As a youngster, I found mathematical word problems especially baffling to solve. Each problem contained just enough of a narrative stem ('Two trains depart from Chicago at precisely 12:23 PM, traveling in opposite directions') to spark my interest, but I never found the main task of 'getting an answer' through arithmetic or algebra very rewarding. Instead, I wanted to think and write about the people on those afternoon trains, speeding away from Chicago and into mystery. In poems, sentences are like that: wonderful locomotives that lead us across landscapes of new thought."

D. A. POWELL was born in 1963 in Albany, Georgia, but has lived most of his life in California. He knows how to hunt, fish, plow, prune, and butcher, but doubts that he could make a living at any of these things. He therefore has taught for a living since 2001. His books include *Chronic* (Graywolf Press, 2009) and *Useless Landscape, or A Guide for Boys* (Graywolf, 2012), recipient of the National Book Critics Circle Award in Poetry.

Powell writes: " 'See You Later.' is part of a series of six-line poems inspired by the language of murder mysteries, along with other forms of puzzles."

ROGER REEVES was awarded a 2013 National Endowment for the Arts fellowship and Ruth Lilly Fellowship. *King Me*, his first book of poems, was published by Copper Canyon Press in 2013. He is an assistant professor of poetry at the University of Illinois at Chicago.

Reeves writes: "'The Field Museum' began when my partner and I took our niece to the Field Museum in Chicago. While folks go to museums with children all the time, the visit was strange and disconcerting for me, because it was the first time that I was in a museum not as a gawker or a man on a reconnaissance mission but as a guardian, as a parental surrogate. I wanted my niece to 'learn' something. But I knew, from past experience with my own parents and guardians, that my self-consciousness could ruin the whole visit. As we walked through the bird wing of the Field Museum, I began to pronounce all the strange bird names, and my niece slowed her hurried pace and became mesmerized as well. I wrote down as many of the bird names as I could. I remembered that in *Crush* Richard Siken had a poem that began as a celebration of names, and I am fascinated with the way lists—grocery lists, to-do lists, rosters—can sound like poems. So the poem began to take shape around the names of the birds—nightjar, grebe, artic loon, pewit—and from the experience of walking with my niece through the museum. I began to think about what it might be like to raise a child, particularly a daughter, without a mother; the fatigue of grief and loss. I created a persona that more fully allowed me to think through the inability to reckon and explain death not only to a child but also to oneself."

Born in the Bronx, New York, in 1954, DONALD REVELL was educated at Harpur College (BA 1975) and the University of Buffalo (PhD 1980). He is the author of twelve collections of poetry, most recently *Tantivy* (2012) and *The Bitter Withy* (2009), both from Alice James Books. He has published six volumes of translations from the French, including Apollinaire's *Alcools* (Wesleyan), Rimbaud's *A Season in Hell* (Omnidawn), Laforgue's *Last Verses* (Omnidawn), and Verlaine's *Songs without Words* (Omnidawn). His critical writings have been collected as *The Art of Attention* (Graywolf) and *Invisible Green: Selected Prose* (Omnidawn). Winner of the PEN USA Translation Award and two-time winner of the PEN USA Award for Poetry, he has also received the Academy of American Poets' Lenore Marshall Prize and is a former Fellow of the Ingram Merrill and Guggenheim Foundations. He has twice been awarded fellowships from the National Endowment for the Arts. A former editor-in-chief of *Denver Quarterly*, he now serves as poetry editor of *Colorado Review*. He is director of graduate studies and professor of English at the University of Nevada, Las Vegas. He lives with his wife, the poet Claudia Keelan, and their children, Benjamin and Lucie, in the Spring Mountains of Nevada.

Of "To Shakespeare," Revell writes: "Since my graduate school days, I've been an ardent if amateur Miltonist. Whenever granted a respite from poetry workshops and thesis guidance, I have opted to teach Milton—in seminars, in surveys, in any academic setting at all. For ten happy years, I fancied myself to be the city of Denver's Municipal Miltonist, offering classes on *Paradise Lost* at both Denver University and the University of Colorado, Denver, often concurrently. When ambition and dollars lured me away to a different city, my students presented me with a beautiful wooden chair, painted all over with images and passages from the clamorous, baroque epic of disobedience and renovation. The chair is my most valued possession.

"About a year ago, a glitch in scheduling found me teaching, for the first time in thirty years, a course in Shakespeare: the Other Poet; the Crowd-Pleaser; the King's Man to my Regicide; the Macy to my Gimbel. And then I was surprised by joy. I cannot speak for the students, but to me, the course became a rapture. I'd chosen to cover the late romances—*Pericles, Cymbeline,* and *The Winter's Tale*—and in them I found such true bliss of reunion and reconciliation, particularly between fathers and their children, that my soul rejoiced. I immediately wrote my poem 'To Shakespeare' in gratitude."

PATRICK ROSAL was born in Belleville, New Jersey, in 1969. He is the author of three full-length collections of poems: *Boneshepherds* (Persea Books, 2011), *My American Kundiman* (Persea, 2006), and *Uprock Headspin Scramble and Dive* (Persea, 2003). A former Fulbright fellow in the Philippines, he teaches in the MFA program at Rutgers University-Camden.

Of "You Cannot Go to the God You Love with Your Two Legs," Rosal writes: "This poem, several years in the making, was triggered by a short passage from the book *On Love* by José Ortega y Gasset, an early-twentieth-century Spanish philosopher. (Ortega y Gasset edited a magazine called *Revista de Occidente* that published the likes of Federico García Lorca and Pablo Neruda.) This is the passage in its entirety: 'You cannot go to the God that you love with the legs of your body, and yet loving Him means going toward Him. In loving we abandon the tranquility and permanence within ourselves, and virtually migrate toward the object. And this constant state of migration is what it is to be in love.'

"It's difficult to remember the exact process, but I think I picked up on the implications of the words 'legs of your body' and 'migration.' One could read that first sentence as having to borrow legs or put into use some legs that aren't of your conventional body. Perhaps one's animal self has another pair of legs that we aren't always aware of. Perhaps the 'constant state of migration' that is the experience of love requires us to engage our animal selves.

"That was the lyric data for the poem's inception. I finished two thirds of the text in early drafts. Perhaps five years later, I completed the poem just as a particularly violent incident was everywhere in the news. The poem has reverberations of particular personal sorrow as well as the public grief of that time."

MARY RUEFLE was born in McKeesport, Pennsylvania, in 1952. Her latest book is *Trances of the Blast* (Wave Books, 2013). Her *Selected Poems* was published in 2010, and a collection of essays, *Madness, Rack, and Honey*, appeared in 2012. She lives in Vermont and teaches in the MFA Program at Vermont College of Fine Arts.

Of "Saga," Ruefle writes: "A friend gave me a copy of one of the great Icelandic sagas; I felt bad that I couldn't finish it, but not so bad that I couldn't write a poem! Another friend told me about the geological rift—some kind of fault line, I suppose—that runs the length of Iceland, and I was struck (once again) by how our human narratives replicate or echo the narratives of our physical planet. On another note, so many things seem both clear and unclear at the same time; can you really *see* what you can *see through*? Of course the poem is not 'about' any of this, but these back thoughts bubble up. And this: all things have to go on much longer than a single story, generations and eons have to pass before anything can be said to have an end."

JON SANDS was born in 1983 in Cincinnati, Ohio. He is a poet, essayist, and the author of *The New Clean* (Write Bloody Publishing, 2011). He starred in the award-winning web series *Verse: A Poetic Murder Mystery* from Rattapallax Films. He is an adjunct with the City University of New York, is a Youth Mentor with Urban Word-NYC, and heads creative writing programs at Bailey House in Harlem (an HIV/AIDS service center) and The Positive Health Project (a syringe exchange center located in Midtown Manhattan). He is the cofounder of Poets in Unexpected Places. He lives in Brooklyn and tours regularly.

Sands writes: "In 'Decoded,' I wanted to produce an effect similar to what you get when you examine a photograph beside its negative. I am struck by how much of what I see in life contains—or is a direct result of—what I don't (or won't) see. There is a blindness, and thus a danger, in privilege, deriving often from what one does not know, or does not wish to know. The creation of the form of this poem helped me to excavate and spotlight ideas or narratives around racial identity that were previously hidden from me. I could not have written 'Decoded' without the work and personhood of Eboni Hogan."

STEVE SCAFIDI was born in Virginia in 1967. He is the author of four books of poetry: *Sparks from a Nine-Pound Hammer* (2001), *For Love of Common Words* (2006), *The Cabinetmaker's Window* (2014), all from LSU Press, and *To the Bramble and the Briar* (University of Arkansas Press, 2014). He works as a cabinetmaker and lives with his family in Summit Point, West Virginia.

Of "Thank You Lord for the Dark Ablaze," Scafidi writes: "This poem took me a few years to write, because I didn't know what I was doing for so long. To write it was to spin and spin and be lost. If you put an irregular or lopsided chunk of wood on the lathe, it will spin and break off if the speed is too high. I had to slow this thing down enough to work on it properly—to understand what I was doing. Once you work that irregular chunk into balance—into a form—then you can speed up the lathe again and it will go beautiful and blurry. I like that. For me, writing poems (and reading them) always involves being lost. I like it that the word 'bewildered' echoes the first syllable in 'wilderness.' I like it that the word 'wilderness' has an anagram for the word 'deer' near the center of it. In this poem that deer is dead and death always bewilders. I write this poem constantly."

FREDERICK SEIDEL was born in St. Louis, Missouri, in 1936. He earned an undergraduate degree at Harvard University in 1957. He is the author of numerous collections of poetry, including *Ooga-Booga* (2006), winner of the *Los Angeles Times* Book Prize; *The Cosmos Trilogy* (2003); and *Going Fast* (1998), all from Farrar, Straus and Giroux.

DIANE SEUSS was born in 1956 in Michigan City, Indiana, and raised in Edwardsburg and Niles, Michigan. Her people are old-school barbers, small-town morticians, telephone operators, nurses, teachers, one-eyed pool players, and furniture salespeople (specializing in the swivel rocker). Her first book, *It Blows You Hollow*, was published by New Issues Press in 1998. Her second collection, *Wolf Lake, White Gown Blown Open*, received the Juniper Prize for Poetry and was published by the University of Massachusetts Press in 2010. Her third book,

Four-Legged Girl, is forthcoming from Graywolf Press in 2015. She is writer-in-residence at Kalamazoo College in Michigan.

Seuss writes: "'Free Beer' represents the crossroads between two seemingly disconnected subjects. I did, as a young child, invite all of the adults in the neighborhood to a puppet show at our home, promising them free beer if they showed up. My father was dying; our family was penniless. We were living on cans of pork and beans delivered in cardboard boxes by the minister of the Fulkerson Park Baptist Church. Needless to say, there was no beer, were no puppets. The show, I guess, was wishful thinking. The intersecting subject that collided with the small narrative of that pocket-sized memory came to me via all of the mass shootings that happened in the United States over the last few years. Did I have the spiritual chops, I wondered, to pray for the bastard perpetrators?

"What happened when the two subjects met in this poem is a mystery I'd prefer not to solve. It's not *about* their intersection, of course, but it's the little song that arose out of their meeting in the puppet theater behind my eyes."

SANDRA SIMONDS was born in Washington, DC, in 1977. She is the author of four books of poetry: *Warsaw Bikini* (Bloof Books, 2009), *Mother Was a Tragic Girl* (Cleveland State University Press, 2012), *The Sonnets* (Bloof, 2014), and *The Glass Box* (forthcoming, Saturnalia Books, 2015). She is assistant professor of English and humanities at Thomas University in Thomasville, Georgia.

Simonds writes: "'I Grade Online Humanities Tests' is a political poem insofar as I tried to write about capitalism, patriarchy, and race without a lot of filter. I wanted to push myself to encounter the limit of the intersection of taboo, autobiography, and art. I wanted to know how much can you say honestly in a poem without your life falling apart? In a sense, this is a response to Auden's assertion that poetry makes nothing happen. Is this true for everyone? Is it true for women? Is it true for people with little power in society? I wanted to investigate the undercurrents of political and sexual power that are just below the surface of everyday life. Can a poem get you fired? Can a poem threaten your marriage? I wanted to see how much power a poem can have when it responds to the fictions of the world."

JANE SPRINGER was born in Lawrenceburg, Tennessee, in 1969. Her two collections of poetry are *Dear Blackbird* (which won the Agha Shahid Ali Prize in 2007) and *Murder Ballad* (Beatrice Hawley Award, 2012). She has received a fellowship from the National Endowment for the Arts and a Whiting Writers' Award. She teaches English and creative writing at Hamilton College in upstate New York, where she lives with her husband, her son, and their three dogs, Leisure-Lee, Azalea, and Woofus.

Of "Forties War Widows, Stolen Grain," Springer writes: "Milton has this remarkable example of epanadiplosis in *Paradise Lost* (Book IV, lines 639–52). I have long admired it, and I wanted to reinvent the technique for the war widows poem by raveling and unraveling synonyms (e.g., spatula becomes utensil), as opposed to repeating words more exactly. My poem also nods to George Herbert's holy 'Easter Wings'— ironic, since the shape of it is evocative of the SR-71 Blackbird war jet from the Cold War era. I hoped to acknowledge the women (those in my family as well as through the ages) who clean up what they can in the harrowing wake of wars past and present."

Corey Van Landingham was born in 1986 in Ashland, Oregon. She is a Wallace C. Stegner Poetry Fellow at Stanford University and is the author of *Antidote* (Ohio State University Press, 2013). She received her MFA from Purdue University, where she was a poetry editor for *Sycamore Review*. She lives in Oakland, California.

Of "During the Autopsy," Van Landingham writes: "While a student at Purdue University, I had the unusual opportunity to visit the cadaver lab for a project my professor, Marianne Boruch, was undertaking. The medical students walked us through the room, showing us various oddities and, with visible glee, watching our reactions. I had the instant urge to liken what I was seeing to something familiar. The bodies were detached from their persons, resulting in a new vision of the body. As a fact. As a warehouse. The cerebellum reminded me of the imprint of a pine-needle cluster. The brain, in my hands, seemed like some dull putty I had handled as a child. The heart was so *meaty*. I began to think about my reaction: was this something only we writers were doing, foreign as we are to the world of the body, more comfortable in language, in metaphor? I wondered whether the medical students, for whom the sight of cadavers may be tedious, ever transform the experience, in their minds, into the sensational, the strange? And so this poem took root there, in that body-clinging smell of the cadaver lab, where I imagined the enchantment, the wonder that I hoped one might find in the routine. I imagined the magic a body could reveal, and how it could become a fulcrum to this one man's very existence. No, to his multitudinous existences."

A poet, playwright, essayist, translator, and actor, AFAA MICHAEL WEAVER (formerly Michael S. Weaver) was born in Baltimore in 1951; he graduated high school and entered the University of Maryland in 1968, when he was sixteen years old. In 1970 he left the university to work in factories for fifteen years. In 1985, he received an NEA fellowship in poetry and the contract for his first book of poems with *Callaloo* at the University of Virginia. In that same year he left factory life to enter Brown University's MFA writing program, where he concentrated on playwriting, and he completed his BA at the University of the State of New York. His thirteen books of poetry include *Water Song* (University Press of Virginia, 1985), *Multitudes* (Sarabande, 2000), *The Plum Flower Dance* (Pittsburgh, 2007), *The Government of Nature* (Pittsburgh, 2013), and *A Hard Summation* (Central Square Press, 2014). He has received a Fulbright appointment (2002) to teach at National Taiwan University and, as a translator, he works with contemporary Chinese poetry. He holds the Alumnae Chair in English at Simmons College and is a visiting faculty member of Drew University's low-residency MFA in poetry and poetry in translation.

Weaver writes: " 'Passing Through Indian Territory' is an American sonnet inspired by my visit in fall 2011 to the University of Oklahoma, where I noticed the presence of cowboys in Oklahoma's history. As a young teenager, I learned a great deal about horses from a maternal uncle. He gave me an Appaloosa filly when I was fourteen years old, the subject of a poem in my early book *My Father's Geography*."

ELEANOR WILNER was born in Cleveland, Ohio, in 1937. She has published seven books of poetry, including *Tourist in Hell* (University of Chicago Press, 2010), *The Girl with Bees in Her Hair* (Copper Canyon, 2004), and *Reversing the Spell: New & Selected Poems* (Copper Canyon, 1998). She coedited with Maurice Manning *The Rag-Picker's Guide to Poetry: Poems, Poets, Process* (University of Michigan, 2013). Her awards include a MacArthur, National Endowment for the Arts, and Pennsylvania Council on the Arts Fellowships, the Juniper Prize, and three Pushcart Prizes. She teaches peripatetically and perennially in the MFA Program for Writers at Warren Wilson College.

Of "Sowing," Wilner writes: "My poems tend to emerge from the imagination, which is to say, I make things up. But this one, uncharacteristically, comes direct from a personal memory, called up by the lines from a poem by Maurice Manning, which became the epigraph: 'I can't make up / a name like Turnipseed, or that // I knew a man who went by such / a goodly name . . . ' And with that name came back, across the years, a young man, my concern about his fate, and with him, a whole era in American history, the crimes and the unthinkable waste resulting from U.S. intervention in Vietnam's war.

"From that name, Turnipseed, the poem emerged: like the disturbance that, as it moves through water, makes the waves, so one association awakened the next, even as Maurice's description of a turnip seed brought on the incommensurate—the immeasurable value of a young man's life, so expendable to the military machine of empire: 'a little bit of hardly anything.'

"A word about the poem's final associative move into the Dreamtime of the West in its last stanza, as the ironic 'bought the farm' expression among soldiers in 'Nam for their dead comrades opened the field to the sowing of a different seed, in the furrow made by the plow of Cadmus in Ovid's retelling of the Greek myths in his *Metamorphoses*.

"As Ovid tells it, Cadmus, who was to found the ill-fated dynasty of Thebes, kills the sacred serpent-dragon of the war god Mars, who has destroyed his company of men. On the instructions of his tutelary goddess Athena, Cadmus ploughs the ground and sows it with the teeth of the dragon, and at once, from this dragon seed, spears arise, then helmets, and soon a field of warriors has risen full grown from the earth, and almost at once it becomes a killing field as they attack one another, until, with only five left, Athena intervenes, peace is made, and Thebes, like Rome, has its origin in brother murder and civil war—all under the red eye of Mars.

"And, though I was not conscious of this when writing, it is obvious now that 'fell like dominoes' refers to the insane justification for the massive carnage, bombing, and defoliation of Vietnam—the theory that if the North Vietnamese won the war, the countries of Southeast Asia would fall to Communism like dominoes. Of course, it was the bodies that fell 'to join the ranks of headstones, *row on row on row . . .* '

"It is my fond hope that Carl Turnipseed survived that bloody war, and, as to the flag-draped coffin, I believe its personal meaning for me in the context of this memory, was such a coffin at the funeral of Waters E. Turpin, my elder colleague at Morgan State, a kind and learned man who put up with my ignorance, and who, the year I was born, 1937, had published the first of his three novels, *These Low Grounds*, which, rare for that time in history, told it like it was."

DAVID WOJAHN was born in St. Paul, Minnesota, in 1953. His eighth collection of poetry, *World Tree*, was published by the University of

Pittsburgh Press in 2011 and was the winner of the Academy of American Poets' Lenore Marshall Poetry Prize. He has received fellowships from the National Endowment for the Arts and the Guggenheim Foundation. His previous collection of poetry, *Interrogation Palace: Selected Poems 1982–2004*, was published by the University of Pittsburgh Press in 2006 and was a named finalist for the Pulitzer Prize and winner of the Folger Shakespeare Library's O. B. Hardison Award. *From the Valley of Making*, a collection of his essays on poetry, will appear from the University of Michigan Press in 2015. He teaches at Virginia Commonwealth University and in the MFA in Writing Program of Vermont College.

Of "My Father's Soul Departing," Wojahn writes: "A few years ago, the poet Michael Waters asked each of a dozen or so poets to translate a work that may be the best known poem of the ancient world, Hadrian's 'Animula.' Legend has it that it was written by the Roman emperor on his deathbed, and in it he bids farewell to his soul. The poem is a lovely bit of leave-taking to his 'body's companion and guest.' The various translations that Michael solicited appeared together in a journal, *The Great River Review*. My version of the poem took several liberties with its content, and I later found myself wondering why I'd turned a work of great tenderness into something considerably more saturnine. 'My Father's Soul Departing' was written in part to answer the question. My father, who died in 1990, was a greatly decent man, but afflicted by many things, not least of which was a lifelong battle with chronic depression and alcoholism. Like so many other children of the depression, he had a difficult childhood, characterized by poverty, an abusive father, a mother afflicted with mental illness, and an education that was cut short in the eighth grade. He served in the army in World War II, and was later employed for many years by the Great Northern Railroad, the creation of the Robber Baron James J. Hill, who nicknamed himself 'The Empire Builder.' And my father was among the last generation of old style Railroad Men. In 1970, he and many of his coworkers were permanently laid off from their positions, and my father's final two decades were characterized by various mental and economic woes.

"The purpose of 'My Father's Soul Departing' is that of almost all elegies—to mourn and to dignify the departed. It's a capsule biography, and the poem is interwoven with passages from my translation of Hadrian's poem. My father was neither an emperor nor an Empire Builder, but one of my projects as a poet has been to do for my father—

in a small way—what potentates have so often done for themselves: that is, to fashion a fitting and lasting memorial."

GREG WRENN was born in Jacksonville, Florida, in 1979. He is the author of *Centaur* (University of Wisconsin Press, 2013) and *Off the Fire Road* (GreenTower Press, 2008). He has received the Brittingham Prize in Poetry and a Stegner Fellowship, as well as awards from the Poetry Society of America and the Bread Loaf Writers' Conference. He is at work on a second full-length collection, *Homeworld*, and a series of essays on coral reefs, climate change, artistic vision, and the impermanence of beauty. A graduate of Harvard University and Washington University in St. Louis, he teaches at Stanford University.

Of "Detainment," Wrenn writes: "Unlike my first book's title poem, in which a man travels to Brazil to be surgically transformed into a centaur, the speaker of 'Detainment'—a suspected terrorist-poet—is kidnapped and brutalized. My aspirations for this poem are wide-ranging: that it express my ambivalence about language's transformative possibilities; ironize the notion that good poems must arise from suffering; and critique the inhumanity of our criminal justice system and the War on Terror, including the practice of extraordinary rendition. An attempt to convey personal as well as national desolation and fragmentation, each of the scattered prose blocks is a kind of cell in which this dispirited, abused voice speaks to itself while in lockdown. For now, his abusers, his torturers, are gone."

ROBERT WRIGLEY was born in East St. Louis, Illinois, in 1951. He is a professor of English at the University of Idaho and lives in the woods, near Moscow, with his wife, the writer Kim Barnes. His most recent books are *Anatomy of Melancholy and Other Poems* (Penguin Books, 2013), and in the United Kingdom, *The Church of Omnivorous Light: Selected Poems* (Bloodaxe Books, 2013).

Of "Blessed Are," Wrigley writes: "On the mountain where I live, wild animals outnumber humans by a considerable margin. I see them a lot, and I write about them a lot, too. I published a book just over a decade ago called *Lives of the Animals*, which ought to have been called, according to a few of my witty friends, 'Deaths of the Animals,' given how many of the poems in that volume looked at, examined, meditated on, and, it seems, endlessly described dead beasts as their subjects. But a subject is not a poem, only the doorway through which the poet enters in search of the poem. Practically speaking, dead animals are easier to examine than living ones. They do not flee; they lie still to be studied. Winter is hard here, too, and among the wild populations are also predators. And they all die, even, I imagine, the ravens, although in all my years of walking through these woods, I have come across every sort of carcass but that of a raven. How can that be? They are highly intelligent birds. They can imitate other birds; they can even imitate human speech. Listening to them, I find it impossible to believe that they communicate less effectively than we do. As for the title and the last word, the less said by me the better."

JAKE ADAM YORK was born in West Palm Beach, Florida, in 1972, and grew up in Gadsden, Alabama. He received a BA in English from Auburn University, and an MFA and PhD in creative writing and English literature from Cornell University. His collections of poetry include *Abide*, published posthumously (Southern Illinois University Press, 2014); *Persons Unknown* (Southern Illinois, 2010); *A Murmuration of Starlings* (Southern Illinois, 2008), which won the Colorado Book Award; and *Murder Ballads* (Elixir Press, 2005), which won the Elixir Prize. He was an associate professor at the University of Colorado, Denver, where he founded the university's creative writing program, as well as the university's national literary journal, *Copper Nickel*. Jake Adam York died suddenly on December 16, 2012, at the age of forty.

DEAN YOUNG was born in Columbia, Pennsylvania, in 1955. He is currently teaching at the University of Texas, Austin. His most recent books are *Fall Higher* (2011) and *Bender* (2012), both by Copper Canyon Press. *The Art of Recklessness* (2010), a book of prose, was published by Graywolf.

Of "Emerald Spider Between Rose Thorns," Young writes: "Like many of my poems, and most poems in general I think, this one is something of a list, a list of phenomena and reaction that may or may not lead to a conclusion. It's not a story, it's an arrangement. I hope to resist narrative and its numbing conventions that depend upon domineering logic, which to my mind is usually insufficient to the full welter of life. We don't live narratives. We hop. I hope this poem conveys a series of amazements in each landing and takeoff. I hope it comes to a sense of an ending that isn't necessarily completion but more like how a song ends, with a sense of sumptuousness achieved."

Rachel Zucker was born during a blizzard in New York City in 1971. She attended Yale and the Iowa Writers' Workshop and then returned to New York. Her nine books include a memoir, *MOTHERs* (Counterpath Press, 2014), and *The Pedestrians* (Wave Books, 2014), a double collection of poetry and prose. *Museum of Accidents* appeared from Wave Books in 2009. She has received a National Endowment for the Arts fellowship and currently teaches poetry at New York University. She has also worked as a labor support doula and a childbirth educator.

Zucker writes: "In 'Mindful,' I write explicitly about my relationship to New York City, where (except for college and graduate school) I've lived for more than forty years. I wanted the poem's form, speed, and diction to mimic New York rather than refer to New York and to pursue a high-population density poetics.

"When I wrote 'Mindful' I'd been listening to podcasts and audio books while traveling alone around the city. I was also using an app that announced my time, distance, and pace when I ran in Central Park. I thought pulling a bubble of sound round me would insulate me from the noise and chaos of the city. I thought RunKeeper would push me to go farther and faster. But rushing around in a moving cloud of narrative, filling all the waking silences, created a mental or emotional implosion. The experience was a more extreme version of my usual daily life in which I am interrupted by my children, my reading, my listening to the swirl of language all around me. I am lucky to have a full life and an active mind, but such fullness is also crazy-making.

" 'Mindful' plays with the recently ubiquitous word 'mindful' as it is used in yoga, parenting, health, and politics. Who doesn't want to be more 'mindful'? If we were all 'mindful,' we'd be slim, compassionate, spiritually centered, environmentally aware Buddhas. One reason I write poetry is that it helps me pay attention to where I am even when I want to escape. I believe in the importance of being present and attentive. I believe in the importance of being present, attentive, 'mindful.' But the catchword doesn't acknowledge the problems of a full mind or the complex ways in which I try to pay more and less attention to the vividness of the world."

MAGAZINES WHERE THE POEMS
WERE FIRST PUBLISHED

ABZ, ed. John McKernan. PO Box 2746, Huntington, WV 25727.

The Academy of American Poets Poem-a-Day, ed. Alex Dimitrov. www.poets.org

AGNI, poetry ed. Lynne Potts. bu.edu/agni

The American Poetry Review, eds. Stephen Berg, David Bonanno, and Elizabeth Scanlon. 320 S. Broad St., Hamilton #313, Philadelphia, PA 19102. www.aprweb.org

The Atlantic, poetry ed. David Barber. www.theatlantic.com

The Awl, poetry ed. Mark Bibbins. www.theawl.com

The Baffler, literary ed. Anna Summers. www.thebaffler.com

Barrow Street, eds. Melissa Hotchkiss, Patricia Carlin, Lorna Blake, and Peter Covino. www.barrowstreet.org/journal

The Believer, poetry ed. Dominic Luxford. www.believermag.com

Birmingham Poetry Review, featured poet editor Gregory Fraser. 1720 2nd Avenue South, HB 203, Birmingham, AL 35294-1260.

Blackbird, eds. Gregory Donovan, Mary Flinn, William Tester. www.blackbird.vcu.edu

Boston Review, poetry eds. Timothy Donnelly and Barbara Fischer. PO Box 425786, Cambridge, MA 02142. www.bostonreview.net

Brilliant Corners, ed. Sascha Feinstein. Lycoming College, 700 College Place, Williamsport, PA 17701.

The Carolina Quarterly, poetry ed. Lee Norton. CB # 3520 Greenlaw Hall, The University of North Carolina, Chapel Hill, NC 27599-3520.

The Cincinnati Review, poetry ed. Don Bogen. PO Box 210069, Cincinnati, OH 45221-0069.

Court Green, eds. CM Borroughs, Tony Triglio, and David Trinidad. Department of Creative Writing, Columbia College, 600 S. Michigan Ave., Chicago, IL 60605.

Crazyhorse, poetry ed. Emily Rosko. crazyhorse.cofc.edu

Cream City Review, poetry eds. Kara van de Graaf and C. McAllister Willams. www.creamcityreview.org

Denver Quarterly, ed. Laird Hunt. University of Denver, Department of English, 2000 E. Asbury, Denver, CO 80208.

FIELD, eds. David Young and David Walker. www.oberlin.edu/ocpress/field

Green Mountains Review, poetry ed. Elizabeth Powell. greenmountains review.com

Gris-Gris, eds. Jay Udall and Scott Banville. www.nicholls.edu/gris-gris

Gulf Coast, poetry eds Patrick Clement James, Michelle Oakes, and Justine Post. gulfcoastmag.org/

The Hampden-Sydney Poetry Review, ed. Nathaniel Perry. Box 66, Hampden-Sydney, VA 23943

Hanging Loose, eds. Robert Hershon, Dick Lourie, and Mark Pawlak. 231 Wyckoff St., Brooklyn, NY 11217.

Harvard Review, poetry ed. Major Jackson. Lamont Library, Harvard University, Cambridge, MA 02138.

Hayden's Ferry Review, poetry eds. Dexter Booth and Hugh Martin. haydensferryreview.blogspot.com/

The Iowa Review, poetry ed. Nikki-Lee Birdsey. 308 EPB, University of Iowa, Iowa City, IA 52242.

jubilat, eds. Kevin González and Caryl Pagel. www.jubilat.org

The Kenyon Review, poetry ed. David Baker. www.kenyonreview.org

The Literary Review, poetry eds. Renée Ashley and Craig Morgan Teicher. www.theliteraryreview.org

Little Patuxent Review, poetry ed. Laura Shovan. littlepatuxentreview.org

London Review of Books, ed. Mary-Kay Wilmers. 28 Little Russell Street, London WC1A 2HN, England.

MAKE Literary Magazine, poetry ed. Joel Craig. makemag.com

MiPOesias, poetry eds. Sarah Blake, Emma Trelles, and Didi Menendez. mipoesias.com

The Missouri Review, poetry ed. Chun Ye. 357 McReynolds Hall, University of Missouri, Columbia, MO 65211.

The Nation, poetry ed. Ange Mlinko. 33 Irving Place, New York, NY 10003.

New Letters, editor-in-chief Robert Stewart. University House, University of Missouri–Kansas City, 5101 Rockhill Road, Kansas City, MO 64110.

The New Yorker, poetry ed. Paul Muldoon. 4 Times Square, New York, NY 10036.

The Normal School, poetry ed. Stacey Balkun. 5245 North Backer Avenue, M/S PB 98, California State University, Fresno, CA 93740-8001.

Painted Bride Quarterly, eds. Kathleen Volk Miller and Marion Wrenn. pbq.drexel.edu

The Paris Review, poetry ed. Robyn Creswell. 544 West 27th St., New York, NY 10001.

Pleiades, poetry eds. Wayne Miller and Kathryn Nuernberger. Department of English, Martin 336, University of Central Missouri, Warrensburg, MO 64093.

Ploughshares, poetry ed. John Skoyles. Emerson College, 120 Boylston St., Boston, MA 02116-4624.

Poet Lore, eds. Jody Bolz and E. Ethelbert Miller. c/o The Writer's Center, 4508 Walsh St., Bethesda, MD 20815.

Poetry, ed. Don Share. poetryfoundation.org/poetrymagazine

Poetry Daily, eds. Don Selby and Diane Boller. www.poems.com

Prairie Schooner, ed. Kwame Dawes. University of Nebraska, 123 Andrews Hall, Lincoln, NE 68588-0334.

A Public Space, poetry ed. Brett Fletcher Lauer. 323 Dean Street, Brooklyn, NY 11217.

Rattle, ed. Timothy Green. 12411 Ventura Blvd., Studio City, CA 91604.

Southern Indiana Review, poetry ed. Marcus Wicker. Orr Center #2009, University of Southern Indiana, 8600 University Blvd., Evansville, IN 47712.

The Southern Review, poetry ed. Jessica Faust. 3rd Floor, Johnston Hall, Louisiana State University, Baton Rouge, LA 70803.

Southwest Review, ed. Willard Spiegelman. PO Box 750374, Dallas, TX 75275-0374.

Spillway, ed. Susan Terris. spillway.org

Terminus Magazine, eds. Katie Chaple and Travis Denton. PO Box 54423, Atlanta, GA 30308.

The Threepenny Review, ed. Wendy Lesser. PO Box 9131, Berkeley, CA 94709.

Tin House, poetry ed. Matthew Dickman. PO Box 10500, Portland, OR 97210.

Tongue, eds. Adam Wiedewitsch, Colin Cheney, and R. A. Villanueva. tongueoftheworld.org

Vinyl Poetry, poetry ed. Phillip B. Williams. vinylpoetry.com

Willow Springs, poetry ed. Kristin Gotch. willowsprings.ewu.edu

ACKNOWLEDGMENTS

The series editor thanks Mark Bibbins for his invaluable assistance. Warm thanks go also to Nora Brooks and Stacey Harwood; to Glen Hartley and Lynn Chu of Writers' Representatives; and to Daniel Burgess, David Stanford Burr, Daniel Cuddy, Ashley Gilliam, Erich Hobbing, and Gwyneth Stansfield at Scribner.

"Priapus" by Alan Dugan (1923–2003), which Terrance Hayes quotes in his introduction, is reprinted with permission. The poem was handed out for critique in the summer of 1992 at the Castle Hill workshop that Dugan ran from 1976 through 2001. Alan Feldman uncovered the poem—in Dugan's hand, not a Xerox—among the papers his daughter, Rebecca, brought home from the workshop. For permission to use the poem, and for their various effort to recover and disseminate it, we are grateful to Keith Althaus and Ezra Shahn, co-executors, estate of Judith Shahn, as well as to Alan Feldman, John Skoyles, and the editors of *Ploughshares*.

For permission to reproduce the diagram by Jacques Maritain that appears in Terrance Hayes's introduction, we are grateful to Princeton University Press: Jacques Maritain, *Creative Intuition in Art and Poetry*. © 1953 Trustees of the National Gallery of Art. Reproduced by permission of Princeton University Press.

Grateful acknowledgment is made of the magazines in which these poems first appeared and the magazine editors who selected them. A sincere attempt has been made to locate all copyright holders. Unless otherwise noted, copyright to poems is held by the individual poets.

Sherman Alexie, "Sonnet, with Pride" from *What I've Stolen, What I've Earned*. © 2013 by Sherman Alexie. Reprinted by permission of Hanging Loose Press. First appeared in *Hanging Loose*.

Rae Armantrout, "Control" from *A Public Space*. Reprinted by permission of the poet.

John Ashbery, "Breezeway" from *The New Yorker*. Reprinted by permission of the poet.

Erin Belieu, "With Birds" from *The Normal School*. Reprinted by permission of the poet.

Linda Bierds, "On Reflection" from *The Atlantic*. Reprinted by permission of the poet.

Traci Brimhall, "To Survive the Revolution" from *The Kenyon Review*. Reprinted by permission of the poet.

Lucie Brock-Broido, "Bird, Singing" from *Stay, Illusion*. © 2013 by Lucie Brock-Broido. Reprinted by permission of Alfred A. Knopf, a division of Random House, Inc. First appeared in *Boston Review*.

Jericho Brown, "Host" from *Vinyl Poetry*. Reprinted by permission of the poet.

Kurt Brown, "Pan Del Muerto" from *Terminus Magazine*. Reprinted by permission.

CAConrad, "wondering about our demise while driving to Disneyland with abandon" from *Denver Quarterly*. Reprinted by permission of the poet.

Anne Carson, "A Fragment of Ibykos Translated 6 Ways" from *London Review of Books*. Reprinted by permission of the poet.

Joseph Ceravolo, "Hidden Bird" from *Collected Poems*. © 2013 by the Estate of Joseph Ceravolo. Reprinted by permission of Wesleyan University Press. Also appeared in *The Nation*.

Henri Cole, "City Horse" from *The Threepenny Review*. Reprinted by permission of the poet.

Michael Earl Craig, "The Helmet" from *jubilat*. Reprinted by permission of the poet.

Philip Dacey, "Juilliard Cento Sonnet" from *New Letters*. Reprinted by permission of the poet.

Olena Kalytiak Davis, "It Is to Have or Nothing" from *Green Mountains Review*. Reprinted by permission of the poet.

Kwame Dawes, "News from Harlem" from *Hayden's Ferry Review* and *Poetry Daily*. Reprinted by permission of the poet.

Joel Dias-Porter, "Elegy Indigo" from *Brilliant Corners*. Reprinted by permission of the poet.

Natalie Diaz, "These Hands, if Not Gods" from *Poets.org*. Reprinted by permission of the poet.

Mark Doty, "Deep Lane" from *Ploughshares*. Reprinted by permission of the poet.

Sean Thomas Dougherty, "The Blues Is a Verb" from *Spillway*. Reprinted by permission of the poet.

Rita Dove, "The Spring Cricket Repudiates His Parable of Negritude" from *Poet Lore*. Reprinted by permission of the poet.

Camille Dungy, "Conspiracy (to breathe together)" from *The American Poetry Review*. Reprinted by permission of the poet.

Cornelius Eady, "Overturned" from *Terminus Magazine*. Reprinted by permission of the poet.

Vievee Francis, "Fallen" from *Prairie Schooner*. Reprinted by permission of the poet.

Ross Gay, "To the Fig Tree on 9th and Christian" from *The American Poetry Review*. Reprinted by permission of the poet.

Eugene Gloria, "Liner Notes for Monk" from *Tongue*. Reprinted by permission of the poet.

Ray Gonzalez, "One El Paso, Two El Paso" from *Barrow Street*. Reprinted by permission of the poet.

Kathleen Graber, "The River Twice" from *Painted Bride Quarterly*. Reprinted by permission of the poet.

Rosemary Griggs, "SCRIPT POEM" from *MAKE Literary Magazine*. Reprinted by permission of the poet.

Adam Hammer, "As Like" from *Pleiades*. Reprinted by permission.

Bob Hicok, "Blue prints" from *The Believer*. Reprinted by permission of the poet.

Le Hinton, "No Doubt About It (I Gotta Get Another Hat)" from *Little Patuxent Review*. Reprinted by permission of the poet.

Tony Hoagland, "Write Whiter" from *The Paris Review*. Reprinted by permission of the poet.

Major Jackson, "OK Cupid" from *Tin House*. Reprinted by permission of the poet.

Amaud Jamaul Johnson, "L.A. Police Chief Daryl Gates Dead at 83" from *Crazyhorse*. Reprinted by permission of the poet.

Douglas Kearney, "The Labor of Stagger Lee: Boar" from *Poetry*. Reprinted by permission of the poet.

Yusef Komunyakaa, "Negritude" from *Gris-Gris*. Reprinted by permission of the poet.

Hailey Leithauser, "In My Last Past Life" from *Southwest Review*. Reprinted by permission of the poet.

Larry Levis, "Elegy with a Darkening Trapeze inside It" from *Blackbird*. Reprinted by permission.

Gary Copeland Lilley, "Sermon of the Dreadnaught" from *MiPOesias*. Reprinted by permission of the poet.

Patrick Rosal, "You Cannot Go to the God You Love with Your Two Legs" from *Gulf Coast*. Reprinted by permission of the poet.

Mary Ruefle, "Saga" from *Court Green*. Reprinted by permission of the poet.

Jon Sands, "Decoded" from *Rattle*. Reprinted by permission of the poet.

Steve Scafidi, "Thank You Lord for the Dark Ablaze" from *ABZ*. Reprinted by permission of the poet.

Frederick Seidel, "To Philip Roth, for His Eightieth" from *London Review of Books*. Reprinted by permission of the poet.

Diane Seuss, "Free Beer" from *The Missouri Review*. Reprinted by permission of the poet.

Sandra Simonds, "I Grade Online Humanities Tests" from *The Awl*. Reprinted by permission of the poet.

Jane Springer, "Forties War Widows, Stolen Grain" from *Birmingham Poetry Review*. Reprinted by permission of the poet.

Corey Van Landingham, "During the Autopsy" from *Antidote*. © 2013 by Corey Van Landingham. Reprinted by permission of Ohio State University Press. First appeared in *The Southern Review*.

Afaa Michael Weaver, "Passing Through Indian Territory" from *The New Yorker*. Reprinted by permission of the poet.

Eleanor Wilner, "Sowing" from *The Hampden-Sydney Poetry Review*. Reprinted by permission of the poet.

David Wojahn, "My Father's Soul Departing" from *AGNI*. Reprinted by permission of the poet.

Greg Wrenn, "Detainment" from *Centaur*. © 2013 by Greg Wrenn. Reprinted by permission of The University of Wisconsin Press. First appeared in *Cream City Review*.

Robert Wrigley, "Blessed Are" from *Southern Indiana Review*. Reprinted by permission of the poet.

Jake Adam York, "Calendar Days" from *The Missouri Review*. Reprinted by permission.

Dean Young, "Emerald Spider Between Rose Thorns" from *Poetry*. Reprinted by permission of the poet.

Rachel Zucker, "Mindful" from *The Pedestrians*. © 2014 by Rachel Zucker. Reprinted with the permission of The Permissions Company, Inc., on behalf of Wave Books. First appeared in *The Kenyon Review*.